THE
POWER
—— OF THE ——
INVISIBLE
FORCES

GLADYS RAJ

ISBN 978-1-0980-4219-6 (paperback)
ISBN 978-1-0980-4220-2 (digital)

Copyright © 2020 by Gladys Raj

All rights reserved. No part of this publication may be reproduced, distributed, or transmitted in any form or by any means, including photocopying, recording, or other electronic or mechanical methods without the prior written permission of the publisher. For permission requests, solicit the publisher via the address below.

Christian Faith Publishing, Inc.
832 Park Avenue
Meadville, PA 16335
www.christianfaithpublishing.com

Printed in the United States of America

CONTENTS

Prefce		5
1	The Unseen Forces	7
2	The Origin of Satan	8
3	The Kingdom of Satan	12
4	The Human Spirit	34
5	The Image of God	37
6	God Created Human Beings as a Triune Being	39
7	The Kingdom of God	40
8	The Redemption Plan of God	44
9	The Power and Supremacy of God	48
10	The Holy Spirit	52
11	Jesus Taught on the Existence of Demons and Cast Them Out of People	53
12	Unseen Supernatural Powers Given to the Followers of Jesus Christ	55
13	Demonic Spirits	57
14	An Open Door to Unseen Evil Forces	82
15	Jesus Is the Way	85
16	Personal Experiences	86
17	Testimonies	88
18	The Power and Authority Over Invisible Forces of Darkness	108
19	Conclusion	110
References		113

PREFCE

I WAS RAISED IN A nominal Christian family. The church I grew up had a form of godliness with no power. Being born in India, I witnessed the manifestation of demonic forces. Most of the Christians, including the church leaders, are not aware of the true working power of the Holy Spirit. Some denominations taught and believed that they don't have to talk about demons as though they don't exist.

The Word of God clearly says, in Hosea 4:6, "My people are destroyed for lack of knowledge."

My family and I were affected by the forces of darkness, although we committed our lives to the Lordship of Jesus Christ. Only after I came to know the full knowledge of the Truth and been baptized in the Holy Spirit was I able to live in victory over the forces of darkness.

In the Last Days, the demonic activities would be increasing. Because of our lack of knowledge, even the modern days, some of the churches have been deceived. Some of them cannot distinguish the manifestation of the powers of Satan and of God. Some of them are not aware how the unseen forces, both the positive and negative ones, operate. Most people do not understand what the devil's power is all about. There are only two forces in this world—God and the devil, good and evil, light and darkness.

It is time for Christians to come to the realization of the counterfeit, as is proclaimed in 2 Corinthians 2:11: "We are not ignorant of his devices." Not only to walk in the power and authority Jesus gave to His followers, but also to set the captives free.

The purpose of this book is to reveal the gospel truth to the people of God and to know how the unseen forces operate in the spiritual realm and in the real world. How can one protect himself or herself from the strategy of the enemy and live a victorious life, exercising the power and authority given to the believers by the authority of the Word of God and by the power of the Holy Spirit? Jesus said in John 8:31–32, "If ye continue in My word, then are ye my disciples indeed: And ye shall know the truth, and the truth shall make you free."

- 1 -

The Unseen Forces

We cannot see, touch, hear, or taste the unseen forces. They are invisible spiritual beings. What we see, touch, hear, and taste, relying on our senses, are not of the real world; they are temporary. The real world is the spiritual world, and it is eternal. The spiritual world is a place we cannot see with our physical eyes. In 2 Corinthians 4:18, we read, "While we look not at the things which are seen, but at the things which are not seen: for the things which are seen are temporal; but the things which are not seen are eternal."

The spiritual beings are not visible to our physical eyes. They are invisible forces, and they have the power. There are two groups of invisible spiritual beings, and they belong to two different kingdoms—the kingdom of God and kingdom of Satan. The angels of God belong to the kingdom of God. The fallen angels, which are also known as the unclean spirits, belong to the kingdom of Satan or the kingdom of darkness. We need to know how these two invisible forces of the kingdom of God and of the kingdom of Satan operate in this world.

– 2 –

The Origin of Satan

The Word says in Isaiah 14:11–15,

> Thy pomp is brought down to the grave, and the noise of thy viols: the worm is spread under thee, and the worms cover thee. How art thou fallen from heaven, O Lucifer, son of the morning! How art thou cut down to the ground, which didn't weaken the nations! For thou hast said in thine heart, I will ascend into heaven, I will exalt my throne above the stars of God: I will sit also upon the mount of the congregation, in the sides of the north: I will ascend above the heights of the clouds: I will be like the most High. Yet thou shalt be brought down to hell, to the sides of the pit.

In Ezekiel 28:12–19, we read,

> Thou full of wisdom, and perfect in beauty. Thou hast been in Eden the garden of God; every precious stone was thy covering, the Sardis, topaz, and the diamond, the beryl, the onyx, and the jasper, the sapphire, the emerald, and the carbuncle, and gold: the workmanship of thy tablets and of thy pipes was prepared in thee in the day

that thou wast created. Thou art the anointed cherub that covereth; and I have set thee so: thou wast upon the holy mountain of a God; thou hast walked up and down in the midst of the stones of fire. Thou wast perfect in thy ways from the day that thou wast created, till iniquity was found in thee. By the multitude of thy merchandise they have filled the midst of thee with violence, and thou hast sinned: therefore I will cast thee as profane out of the mountain of God: and I will destroy thee, O covering cherub, from the midst of the stones of fire. Thine heart was lifted up because of thy beauty, thou hast corrupted thy wisdom by reason of thy brightness: I will cast thee to the ground, I will lay thee before kings, that they may behold thee. Thou hast defiled thy sanctuaries by the multitude of thine iniquities, by the iniquity of thy traffick; therefore will I bring forth a fire from the midst of thee, it shall devour thee, and I will bring thee to ashes upon the earth in the sight of all them that behold thee. All they that know thee among the people shall be astonished at thee: thou shalt be a terror, and never shall thou be any more.

And in Revelation 12:4, 9–10, we read this:

> And his tail drew the third part of the stars of heaven, and did cast them to the earth and the dragon stood before the woman which was ready to be delivered, for to devour her child as soon as it was born. And the great dragon was cast out, that old serpent, called the Devil, and Satan, which deceiveth the whole world: he was cast out into the earth and his angels were cast out with him. And I heard a loud voice saying

> in heaven, Now is come salvation, and strength, and the kingdom of our God, and the power of his Christ: for the accuser of our brethren is cast down, which accused them before our God day and night.

Lucifer was an archangel, a created being not equal with God, who sought to elevate himself to a position of equality with God. He considered himself very wise, beautiful, glorious, and thought himself that he could be equal with God. Pride entered his heart.

God created all things and the entire universe by the power of His spoken word, except for human beings. God created the angels to worship Him. One of the angels named Lucifer was the most beautiful, most powerful, wisest, most perfect, and most sinless being from the day he was created. Lucifer was appointed as a worship leader, the anointed cherub to lead the angels to worship God, the Creator of the universe. As the anointed cherub, Lucifer was given the privilege of standing in the presence of God. As long as Lucifer chose to do the will of God, there was no evil in the universe. He was named the son of the morning. He was elevated to a special and privileged position before the throne of God. His very garments were made of precious stones, reflecting the glory of the trinity.

The day came when Lucifer, the archangel, caused rebellion in heaven. He corrupted his wisdom, and because of his beauty, he became proud and wanted to be like God. He desired to be worshipped rather than worshipping God. He was a powerful angel who became perverted and rebelled against God. He influenced one-third of the angels to follow him and battle the Almighty. Not content with the beautiful and intelligence God gave him and his prestige as God's angels, he aspired to be equal with God.

As soon as he chose to follow his own will, he persuaded others to follow him in a great rebellion against the authority of God. As a result, he was thrown out of heaven, along with the one-third of the angels who followed him and rebelled against God. The one-third of the angels who followed him were once beautiful, heavenly beings surrounding the throne of God. Since they rebelled against God with Lucifer, they became unclean spirits and known as fallen angels.

Lucifer was hence known as Satan, and the angels followed him were hence known as the devils or demons. Because they lost their position in heaven and the fallen spirits lost their beauty. They are angry with God. Their prime motive is to destroy what God loves or creates. Since God loves the human race more than anything else, they wish to hurt and destroy it. God threw Lucifer and his followers, one-third of the angels, out because only holiness is allowed in heaven.

The demons cannot be seen with human eyes. As fallen spirits, they desire to dwell in a human's or animal's body in order to manifest themselves.

– 3 –

The Kingdom of Satan

God of This World

THE BIBLE IN 2 Corinthians 4:4 says, "In whom the god of this world hath blinded the minds of them which believe not, lest the light of the glorious gospel of Christ, who is the image of God, should shine unto them." Satan is called the god of this world. He is not the Creator; he is a created being. He is not omnipotent, omniscient, or omnipresent.

As the god of this world, Satan blinds the minds of unbelievers from receiving the truth. He tempts and deceitfully instigates them to sin and hinders them to come to know the knowledge of truth of the Gospel of Jesus Christ. He deceives the Christians who do not have the full knowledge in the Word of God. He perverts and compromises the word of God. The Gospel of Jesus Christ is the Good News, that God Himself came into this world as a human being and defeated Satan and made a way for those who surrendered their lives to the Lordship of Jesus to be transformed from the kingdom of Satan to Kingdom of God (Col. 1:13).

In Luke 4:5–7, we read this:

> And the devil taking Him [Jesus] up into an high mountain, showed unto him all the kingdoms of the world in a moment of time. And the devil said unto Him, all this power will I give thee and the glory of them for that is delivered

unto me and to whomsoever I will I give it. If thou therefore will worship me all shall be thine. And Jesus answered and said unto him, Get thee behind me Satan for it is written, thou shalt worship the Lord thy God, and Him only shalt thou serve.

Satan tried to tempt Jesus and told Him, "All this power will I give thee and the glory of them for that is delivered unto me and to whomsoever I will give it." The power was not given to him, but he deceived Adam and Eve in the garden of Eden and took what God entrusted to them by lying to them.

How Satan Became God of This World

We read these verses from the Book of Genesis:

1. Genesis 1:26–28: "And God said, Let us make man in our image after our likeness and let them have dominion over the fish of the sea, and over the fowl of the air, and over the cattle, and over all the earth, and over every creeping thing that creepeth upon the earth. So God created man in His own image, in the image of God created He him, male and female created He them. And God blessed them, and God said unto them, be fruitful, and multiply, and replenish the earth and subdue it and have dominion over the fish of the sea, and over the fowl of the air, and over every living thing that moveth upon the earth."
2. Genesis 2:7–9: "And the Lord God formed man of the dust of the ground, and breathed into his nostrils the breath of life; and man became a living soul. And the Lord God

planted a garden eastward in Eden: and there he put the man whom he had formed. And out of the ground made the Lord God to grow every tree that is pleasant to the sight, and good for food: the tree of life also in the midst of the garden, and the tree of knowledge of good and evil."

3. Genesis 2:15–17: "And the Lord God took the man, and put him into the garden of Eden to dress it and to keep it. And the Lord God commanded the man, saying of every tree of the garden thou mayest freely eat: but of the tree of the knowledge of good and evil, thou shalt not eat of it: for in the day that thou eatest thereof thou shalt surely die."

4. Genesis 2:21–22: "And the Lord God caused a deep sleep to fall upon Adam, and he slept and he took one of his ribs, and closed up the flesh instead thereof; and the rib, which the Lord God had taken from man, made he a woman, and brought her unto the man."

5. Genesis 3:1–6: "Now the serpent was more subtle than any beast of the field which the Lord God had made. And he said unto the woman, yea, hath God said, ye shall not eat of every tree of the garden? And the woman said unto the serpent, we may eat of the fruit of the trees of the garden: but of the fruit of the tree which is in the midst of the garden, God hath said, ye shall not eat of it, neither shall ye touch it, lest ye die. And the serpent said unto the woman, ye shall not surely die: for God doth know that in the day ye eat thereof, then your eyes shall be opened, and ye shall be as gods, knowing

good and evil. And when the woman saw that the tree was good for food, and that it was pleasant to the eyes, and a tree to be desired to make one wise, she took of the fruit thereof, and did eat, and gave also unto her husband with her and he did eat."

God created male and female in His own image. "In His own image" means not the outward appearance but the free will to act upon with God's perfection and righteousness. God's own creative life and power were breathed into them. God gave them the power and authority to rule and reign with God as His earthly representatives. They were filled with God's authority, His dominion, and His love from the day of their creation for all eternity.

God created all things under the sky for Adam and Eve to enjoy the fruits of all the trees, except the fruit of one tree which gave the knowledge of good and evil. God warned them that if they eat the fruit of that tree, they would die. Therefore, He commanded them not to eat the fruit of that tree which gives knowledge of the good and evil.

But Satan disguised himself in the form of a serpent and approached Eve and tempted her and told her that the day she eats the fruit of that tree, which God had forbidden them to eat, that they would become like God. First of all, Satan wanted to become like God. When he was thrown out and lost his position, he tempted Eve to become like God. Satan gained access to Adam's and Eve's minds. He attacked Eve's mind as a serpent and put doubt into Eve's mind. He knew that God had commanded Adam and Eve not to eat from the tree of knowledge of good and evil, but he tried to plant doubt in Eve's mind. He wanted her to question God's Word.

This first mistake Eve made eventually led her to sin by listening to Satan. He lied to Eve. He contradicted God's word. He told her that she would not die if she ate the forbidden fruit. Eve not only listened to Satan; she carried on a conversation with him. Both Adam and Eve knew what God had commanded them concerning the forbidden fruit. They knew God had told them that if they ate of the fruit, they would die.

Satan caused Eve to doubt God's word, and instead of rejecting Satan's lies, she acted upon Satan's suggestion. She kept looking at the fruits of that tree. The more she looked, the more she was convinced of what Satan suggested to her. She not only ate the fruit but also gave it to her husband. Instead of correcting her, Adam too ate of the fruit. Thus they both willingly disobeyed God and fell into Satan's trap of death and destruction. Since they did what Satan suggested, disobeying God's instruction, they put themselves under Satan's control and lost their God-given power and authority and dominion over earth. Through deception, Satan thus got the power and authority of the system of this world and became the god of this world. Since they did what Satan suggested, they not only put themselves under the power and control of Satan, but they also broke their fellowship with God. Thus sin entered the earth and Satan became the god of this world, and the separation took place between God and mankind. They did not die physically, but they died spiritually and they did not see God anymore.

The first thing Adam and Eve experienced was fear. Then came the guilt, shame, and blame. Up until that time, they were innocent and they did not know what fear, guilt, and shame was. When God called out to Adam, he was afraid, and they both hid themselves. Also they were ashamed. They covered themselves with fig leaves because they were naked. Jesus said, "To whom you obey you become the servant."

John 8:34 says, "Verily, verily, I say unto you, whosoever committeth sin is the servant of sin."

There are two forces—the forces of God and the forces of Satan. God is love, and Satan is full of hatred. God is holy and righteous, whereas Satan is unholy and the author of wickedness and evil. God is light, and Satan is the prince of the power of the darkness. God is the truth, and Satan is a liar. Jesus is the prince of peace.

Jesus is making it clear in "Whom we obey we become the servant" that if we obey God's ways and His commandments, we will come under His protection and His Kingdom. However, if we disobey God's commandments and follow Satan's ways of wickedness and evil, then we will come under his control and rulership. When we commit sin and live in the ways of Satan, it will give him the legal right over us. He will entice and deceive and trap the person, and once the person comes under his rulership, he will then bring all kinds of heartaches and pains and afflictions in every possible way and cause the people to blame God.

Satan, the Prince of the Power of the Air

In Ephesians 2:2, we read, "Wherein in time past ye walked according to the course of this world, according to the prince of the power of the air the spirit that now worketh in the children of disobedience."

As "prince of the power of the air," Satan is a ruler over the evil powers and principalities of the darkness of this world. He is the prince of demons, which make up his kingdom. He has set up his headquarters somewhere between heaven and earth, which is called the firmament. He works through the evil spirits under his command and through the "children of disobedience," those who are not followers of Jesus Christ.

Even today, Satan, as the prince of the power of the air, commissions evil spirits to oppress and torment God's people. Satan does not want to be exposed. He sends spirits of fear, hate, lust, greed, doubt, confusion, and a multitude of other negative forces to attack people, especially God's people.

Ephesians 6:12 reads, "For we wrestle not against flesh and blood, but against principalities, against powers, against the rulers of the darkness of this world, against spiritual wickedness in high places."

Satan operates his kingdom of darkness like an organized army. The devil and demons abode and operate in the heavens above the earth. Apostle Paul mentions the group of evil spirits who operate according to their ranking order. The "first principalities" (the "below principalities") are the "powers," "rulers of the darkness of this world," and "spiritual wickedness in high places." Satan gives them orders and assignments and then sends them out his soldiers to destroy, destruct, possess, vex, deceive, and to kill human beings.

The ultimate plan and purpose of the kingdom of Satan is to attack and destroy humanity. Their objective is to tear down and destroy all that is holy, all that is pure, and all that is moral. Their objective is to bring division and strife within churches and families and to rob their joy and peace. He is a rival of God. He cannot fight God, so he fights everything of God.

Thus, our battle today is not against Satan (the devil) alone but against Satan and all the fallen angels (demons). The Scripture says our battle is with the rulers—not with one ruler (Satan) but against *powers* and *principalities* (plural). Hence, our battle today is against the devil and all his evil forces, the demons. These demonic powers control the darkness of the earth's atmosphere. They do not live in the third heaven, which is the home of God, the angels, and the righteous. God ejected them out from heaven above. They live in the firmament, the place above the earth.

Prince of This World

In John 12:31, we read, "Jesus said, now is the judgement of this world: now shall the prince of this world be cast out."

Jesus was referring to Satan as the "prince of this world." As prince of this world, Satan is not in control of the world. God has not given him the power and authority to exercise dominion over it. As "prince of this world," Satan does not have dominion and control over believers. Before Jesus went to the cross, He told His disciples, "Now shall the prince of this world be cast out." The very moment Jesus rose from the dead, Satan was cast out. It does not mean he was cast out of this world or that he no longer is at work on earth. But the power Satan had over men was broken by the power of the blood of Jesus Christ which was shed at Calvary.

Colossians 2:14–15 says, "Blotting out the handwriting of ordinances that was against us, which was contrary to us, and took it out of the way, nailing it to his cross: and having spoiled principalities and powers, he made a show of them openly, triumphing over them in it."

The power of Satan was nailed to the cross. Those who believe and surrender their lives to the Lordship of Jesus Christ are delivered from the power and control of Satan and transformed into the kingdom of God.

As prince of this world, Satan is a ruler and exercises power and dominion only over the unbelievers who are in this world and the evil world system he has organized. As the prince of this world, he works in and through those who yielded to him. Thus they become part of his kingdom of darkness. Being a spiritual being, Satan cannot operate on his own. He is looking for human bodies, and he will work through those who yield to him.

> And you, being dead in your sins and the uncircumcision of your flesh. (Col. 2:13)

As prince of this world, Satan controls and exercises power over those who are not committed their lives to the Lordship of Jesus. He blinds the mind of those who are not under the Lordship of Jesus and incarcerates them. So they become the part of his kingdom of darkness, and he controls their mind and have dominion over them.

> Wherein in time past ye walked according to the course of this world, according to the *prince of the power of the air* [emphasis mine], the spirit that now worketh in the children of disobedience. (Eph. 2:2)

As "prince of the power of the air," Satan is a ruler over the evil powers and principalities of the darkness of this world. He is the prince of demons, the latter of which makes up his kingdom. He sets up his headquarters somewhere between heaven and earth. As the "prince of the power of the air," Satan commissions evil spirits to oppress and torment God's people. He sends spirits of fear, hate, lust, greed, doubt, confusion, and a multitude of other spirits to attack people.

Satan is not omnipresent; he cannot be in more than one place at a time or omniscient like God; his powers are limited. He, therefore, works through the evil and wicked spirits through the fallen angels under his command and through the "children of disobedience"—that is, those who are not followers of Jesus Christ. Those who have not totally surrendered their lives to the Lordship of Jesus Christ come under the control and power of Satan. As the prince of the power of the air, he influences them and causes them to disobey God. Since they have no physical form, they seek to indwell humans or animals (as in the case of the swine at Gadara in Matthew 12:45), but humans are preferred. Satan may attack through the mind, body, or soul and seek to destroy human being mentally, physically, and spiritually. Satan is also referred to as god of this world, which means he is the god of the system of this world and those who make him their god who worship Baal or creation or other idol gods.

"As the "prince of the power of the air," Satan commissions evil spirits to oppress and torment even the followers of Christ. He sends spirits of fear, hate, lust, greed, doubt, confusion, and all other negative forces to attack the believers.

> Hereafter I will not talk much with you for the *prince of this world* [emphasis mine] cometh, and hath nothing in me. (John 14:30)

Jesus knew that the "prince of the world," Satan, was coming. He knew Satan was going to do everything he could in an attempt to destroy God's plan of redemption. Jesus knew that when He died, Satan would be cast out and his works and his power over man would be broken. Satan was defeated at Calvary. Satan no longer has any power over those who surrendered their lives to the Lordship of Jesus.

> Nevertheless I tell you the truth; it is expedient for you that I go away: for if I go not away, the Comforter (the Holy Spirit) will not come

> unto you; but if I depart, I will send Him unto you. And when He is come, He will reprove the world of sin, and of righteousness, and of judgment: of sin, because they believe not on me; of righteousness, because I go to my Father, and ye see me no more; of judgement, because the *prince of this world* [emphasis mine] is judged. (John 16:7–11)

Satan was an archangel and the worship leader. He has more power than the human being. Therefore, Jesus said, "It is expedient that I go away and send the Holy Spirit unto you." Once the Holy Spirit has come, He will reprove the world of sin and of righteousness. Because Jesus crushed on the cross Satan's grip on humanity's sin and having been defeated, Satan is judged.

Character and Strategy of Satan

> Jesus said, The thief [emphasis mine] does not come except to steal, and to kill, and to destroy. (John 10:10)

Jesus exposed Satan's characteristics. Jesus referred him as a thief. He is the rival of God. His character is exactly opposite to God. God is love; whereas, Satan is full of hatred. God is truth, and Satan is a liar and in him there is no truth. He operates bringing division, strife, confusion, fear, terror, shame, guilt, and deception. He is a murderer, violator, rebellious, accuser, and evil.

His strategy is to hinder God's will from being fulfilled on earth. He is seeking to destroy God's work and human's life. With deception and lies, he blinds the people from seeing the truth. He corrupts the minds of people and turns their hearts away from God. He has brought sin, sickness, destruction, and death into the world. His goal and purpose is to rob, kill, and to destroy people whom God created and whom God loves.

> And when the *tempter* [emphasis mine] came to Him [Jesus], he said, if thou be the Son of God, command that these stones be made bread. But He answered and said, it is written, man shall not live by bread alone, but by every word that proceedeth out of the mouth of God. (Matt. 4:3)

Satan is a tempter. Jesus was sent forth and commissioned by God to defeat Satan and to take back what was stolen from Adam and Eve in the Garden of Eden. Satan knew who Jesus was. He tried to tempt and made an attempt to stop Him from fulfilling God's will.

> And I heard a loud voice saying in heaven, Now is come salvation and strength, and the kingdom of our God, and the power of his Christ for the *accuser* [emphasis mine] of our brethren is cast down, which accused them before our God day and night. (Rev. 12:10)

Satan is an accuser and a slanderer. Although Satan fell from his exalted position and was cast out of God's presence, he still has access into the heavenlies where he appears before God to bring accusations against God's people, night and day. Satan appeared before God and brought accusation against Job (Job 1:6–12). One of Satan's characteristics is accusing God's children before God and bringing accusations and slandering God before men.

> And the great dragon was cast out, that old serpent, called the Devil, and Satan, which *deceiveth* [emphasis mine] the whole world: he was cast out into the earth, and his angels were cast out with him. (Rev. 12:9)

Satan is a deceiver. He often appears as having the truth and deceives many. Satan often blinds the lost by giving them a heavenly way to go to hell. In other words, religion is Satan's substitute for the Gospel. He cause people not to believe the Gospel truth. He deceives people to believe that he does not exist so that they will not resist his assaults.

> Ye are of your father the devil, and the lusts of your father ye will do. He was a murderer from the beginning, and abode not in the truth, because there is no truth in him. When he speaketh a lie, he speaketh of his own for he is a liar, and the father of it. (John 8:44)

Satan is a liar and a murderer. He hates truth and hinders people from knowing the truth. He blinds the hearts and minds of unbelievers so they will be unable to see the truth. He lies and deceives the unbelievers and cause them to worship the idols and creation rather than the Creator. The unbelievers are those who do not know Jesus and not committed their lives to the Lordship of Jesus. The believers are those who know Jesus as their personal Savior and committed their lives to the Lordship of Jesus. Satan lies and deceives even the believers, the Christians, and cause them to doubt God's promises.

> Be sober, be vigilant: because your adversary the devil, as a roaring lion, walketh about, seeking whom he may devour. (1 Pet. 5:8)

Peter described Satan as our adversary, the one who fights and opposes us. As our adversary, Satan is going to and fro upon the earth as a lion stalking its prey, seeking those he can seize and bring to destruction. Since he is a spirit being, he usually works through people to oppose godly people.

Throughout Jesus's life, Satan (as Jesus's adversary) worked through people to oppose and attack Him. When Jesus was born, Satan worked through Herod and tried to kill him by ordering all the male children two years of age and under to be killed (Matt. 2:16). As He ministered and taught in the synagogues, Jesus was opposed by the Jewish leaders. His real adversary was not the Jewish leaders or the Roman soldiers who beat and mocked Him and nailed Him to the cross, not even Judas or Herod or Pilate. His real adversary was Satan, working through them.

As we can see, Satan is a deceiver, liar, accuser, and murderer and he tempts people to do what is not right in the sight of God and cause them to disobey Him. Satan has many names, such as dragon, serpent, adversary, Belial, Beelzebub, god of this world, ruler of the darkness of this world, and prince of the power of the air, among many others. He is mentioned in the Bible at least 175 times. He twists God's word and substitutes with false religion and false doctrines. He hates God and God's people.

One of Satan's major activities upon the earth today is to oppose to fight and wage war against God's people and all that is holy and righteous. The moment we begin to do the work that God has given us to do, Satan, our adversary, will be there to oppose us. It is not the people but Satan using the people to attack and oppose God's people. It is a war not of the flesh but of the Spirit.

Satan Tempts, Instigates, and Deceives People to Disobey God's Commandments

The first commandment of God was to worship Jehovah, the Creator of heaven and earth, and Him only. The worship of creatures is forbidden. It is forbidden to make any image or picture of a deity in any form or to worship any creature, image, idol, or picture.

We read these from the Word:

> Thou shalt have no other gods before me. Thou shalt not make unto thee any graven image, or any likeness of any thing that is in heaven above, or that is in the earth beneath, or that is in the water under the earth. Thou shalt not bow down thyself to them, nor serve them. (Exod. 20:3–5)

And the Lord said unto Moses, go, get thee down, for thy people, which thou brightest out of the land of Egypt, have corrupted themselves. They have turned aside quickly out of the way which I commanded them, they have made them a molten calf, and have worshipped it, and have sacrificed thereunto, and said, these be thy gods, O Israel, which have brought thee up out of the land of Egypt. And the Lord said unto Moses, I have seen this people, and, behold, it is a stiff-necked people. (Exod. 32:7–9)

Unto thee it was showed, that thou mightiest know that the Lord He is God; there is none else beside Him. (Deut. 4:35)

Thou shalt have none other gods before me. Thou shalt not make thee any graven image, or any likeness of any thing that is in heaven above, or that is in the earth beneath, or that is in the waters beneath the earth: Thou shalt not bow down thyself unto them, nor serve them: for I the Lord thy God am a jealous God, visiting the iniquity of the fathers upon the children unto the third and fourth generation of them that hate me. And shewing mercy unto thousands of them that love me and keep my commandments. (Deut. 5:7–10)

Ye shall not go after other gods, of the gods of the people which are round about you. (Deut. 6:14)

With whom the Lord had made a covenant, and charged them, saying, ye shall not fear other gods, nor bow yourselves to them, nor serve them, nor sacrifice to them. But the Lord, who brought you up out of the land of Egypt with great power and a stretched out arm, Him shall ye fear, and Him shall ye worship, and to Him shall ye do sacrifice. (2 Kings 17:35–36)

There shall no strange god be in thee: neither shalt thou worship any strange god. (Ps. 81:9)

I am the LORD: that is my name: and my glory will I not give to another, neither my praise to graven images. (Isa. 42:8)

Ye are my witnesses, saith the Lord, and my servant whom I have chosen; that ye may know and believe me and understand that I am he: before me there was no God formed, neither shall there be after me. I even I, am the Lord; and beside me there is no savior. (Isa. 43:10–11)

Thus saith the Lord the King of Israel, and his redeemer the Lord of hosts; I am the first, and I am the last: and beside me there is no God. (Isa. 44:6)

I am the Lord, and there is none else, there is no God beside me: I girded thee, though thou hast not known me: that they may know from the rising of the sun, and from the west, that there is none beside me. I am the Lord and there is none else. For thus saith the Lord that created the heavens; God himself that formed the earth and made it; he hath established it, he created it not in vain, he formed it to be inhabited: I am the Lord; and there is none else. Tell ye, and bring them near; yea, let them take counsel together who hath declared this from ancient time? who hath told it from that time? have not I the Lord? and there is no God else beside me; a just God and a Savior; there is none beside me. Look unto me, and be ye saved, all he ends of the earth: for I am God, and there is none else. (Isa. 45:5–6, 18, 21–22)

Remember the former things of old: for I am God, and there is none else; I am God, and there is none like me. (Isa. 46:9)

And go not after other gods to serve them, and to worship them and provoke me not to anger with the works of your hands. (Jer. 25:6)

They have set up kings, but not by me: they have made princes, and I knew it not: of their silver and their gold have they made them idols, that they may be cut off. (Hosea 8:4)

Yet I am the Lord thy God from the land of Egypt, and the shalt know no god but me for there is no savior beside me. (Hosea 13:4)

For there be that are called gods, whether in heaven or in earth [as their gods and lords are many], but to us there is but one God, the Father, of whom are all things, and we in Him; and one Lord Jesus Christ, by whom are all things, and we by Him. (1 Cor. 8:5–6)

But I say, that the things which the Gentiles sacrifice, they sacrifice to devils, and not to God: and I would not that ye should have fellowship with devils. (1 Cor. 10:20)

Little children, keep yourselves from idols. (1 John 5:21)

And the rest of the men which were not killed by these plagues yet repented not of the works of their hands, that they should not worship devils, and idols of gold, and silver, and brass, and stone, and of wood: which neither can see, nor hear, nor walk. (Rev. 9:20)

Time and time again, God, the Creator of heaven and earth, commanded man to worship Him and Him alone and to give Him the first place. He commanded not to worship or to bow down to any creation, creature, or any man-made image or idols. God forbade the making of any graven images or bowing down to other gods. He also commanded us to give Him the priority and first place and that nothing should take His place. Those who worship idols and creations rather than the true Living God come under curse. They will be cursed for three or four generations. At the same time, those who worship the true Living God and those who give Him the first place in their lives will be blessed for a thousand generations.

God appointed Satan, Lucifer, the fallen archangel to be the worship leader. But when pride and iniquity entered Satan's heart, he desired to be worshipped rather than worship God. He rebelled; and as a result he lost his position, his beauty, and was thrown out, along of a third of the demons who followed him. Ever since he long to be worshipped, he corrupted the minds and hearts of the people to turn away from worshipping the Almighty Living God, who created the heaven and earth. He blinds the people's mind and cause them to believe and embrace the creation, creature, and man-made idols and images as their gods and to worship them.

Satan rebelled against God and even today tempts people to rebel and cause those who believe in him to blame God. He tempted Adam and Eve in the garden of Eden, and deceived them, and caused them to disobey God. First of all, he wanted to be like God and tempted Adam and Eve that they will become like God when they eat the fruit, which God forbidden. As a result, separation took place between Holy God and Adam and Eve, who committed sin against God. Then on one to all, who came into this world, were born as a sinner and through sin, a wall between God and mankind was built.

Ephesians 2:13–18 reads this:

> But now in Christ Jesus ye who sometimes were far off are made nigh by the blood of Christ. For he is our peace, who hath made both one, and hath broken down the middle wall of partition between us; having abolished in his flesh the enmity, even the law of commandments contained in ordinances; for to make in himself of twain one new man, so making peace; and that he might reconcile both unto God in one body by the cross, having slain the enmity thereby: and came and preached peace to you which were afar off, and to them that were nigh. For through him we both have access by one Spirit unto the Father.

We also read this in 2 Corinthians 5:17–18, 21:

> Therefore if any man be in Christ, he is a new creature: old things are passed away; behold, all things are become new. And all things are of God, who hath reconciled us to himself by Jesus Christ, and hath given to us the ministry of reconciliation; for He hath made Him to be sin for us, who knew no sin; that we might be made the righteousness of God in Him.

God is love, holy, righteous, omnipotent, omniscient, and omnipresent. No human can reach Him because none can meet His standard of holiness and righteousness. Therefore, He sent His Son—that is, God Himself came into this world in the form of a man and made a way for atonement and made a way for mankind to meet and communicate with the Creator through His Son, Jesus Christ. God reconciled the world to Himself through His Son, Jesus Christ, who paid the penalty by dying on the Cross for the sins of the world and who broke down the wall between human being and God.

Satan deceived Adam and Eve and stole the power and authority given to them and became the God of the system of this world. God is truthful to His word. His only begotten son came into this world as a human being, left behind heaven, and defeated Satan. Satan tried to trap Him in many ways, but Satan could not succeed. Jesus was born with no human relationships, with no sin, and shed every drop of His blood to take away the sins of this world and defeat Satan and take back the keys, which was stolen by Satan.

Second Corinthians 4:4 says, "In whom the god of this world hath blinded the minds of them which believe not."

Even today in the twenty-first century, in spite of advanced technology and higher education (including doctors, engineers, scientists), we are still blinded and deceived by Satan. They worship stones, cows, snakes, dragons, trees, sun, moon, so-called prophets, human beings, man-made idols, images, pictures, and bow down to them as their gods. They are sincere in their heart, and Satan blinded their eyes in such a way that they truly believe them as their gods and spend time in worshipping, meditating, and sacrificing to those creations and creatures.

When they worship and make sacrifices to those idols, creations, and creatures; they are worshipping Satan and not the true God. Satan lies to the people and makes them to think that they are pleasing God, and they are no longer aware that they are worshipping Satan and displeasing the true Living God. As the god of this world, Satan has the ability to blind the minds of the people who do not know Jesus from receiving the truth of the Gospel of Jesus Christ. One can worship the true Living God only through His Son, Jesus Christ, who made atoned for the sins of the world. Jesus, who committed no sin, died on the Cross to take away the sins of mankind. On the third day, He rose again and restored the relationship between God and human beings.

THE POWER OF THE INVISIBLE FORCES

Possession of Unseen Forces in the Human Body

We read in Mark 5:2–20,

> And when he was come out of the ship, immediately there met Him out of the tombs a man with an unclean spirit. Who had his dwelling place among the tombs; and no man could bind him, no, not with chains. Because that he had been often bound with fetters and chains, and the chains had been plucked asunder by him, and the fetters broken in pieces: neither could any man tame him. And always, night and day, he was in the mountains, and in the tombs, crying, and cutting himself with stones.
>
> But when he saw Jesus afar off, he ran and worshipped him, and cried with a loud voice and said, what have I to do with thee, Jesus, thou Son of the most high God? I adjure thee by God, that thou torment me not. For he said unto him, Come out of the man, thou unclean spirit. And he asked him, What is thy name? And he answered, saying, My name is Legion: for we are many. And he besought him much that he would not send them away out of the country. Now there was there nigh unto the mountains a great herd of swine feeding. And all the devils besought him, saying, Send us into the swine, that we may enter into them. And forthwith Jesus gave them leave. And the unclean spirits went out, and entered into the swine: and the herd ran violently down a steep place into the sea, (they were about two thousand;) and were choked in the sea.
>
> And they that fed the swine fled, and told it in the city, and in the country. And they went out to see what it was that was done. And they came

> to Jesus, and see him that was possessed with the devil, and had the legion, sitting, and clothed, and in his right mind: and they were afraid. And they that saw it told them how it befell to him that was possessed with the devil, and also concerning the swine. And they began to pray him to depart out of their coasts. And when he was come into the ship, he that had been possessed with the devil prayed him that he might be with him. Howbeit Jesus suffered him not, but saith unto him, Go home to thy friends, and tell them how great things the Lord hath done for thee, and hath had compassion on thee. And he departed, and began to publish in Decapolis how great things Jesus had done for him: and all men did marvel.

The unclean spirit caused the man to turn totally insane and ruled over him by possessing his body, soul, and mind. In this story, we see the unclean sprit made the man live worse than an animal. His dwelling was among the tombs. And always, night and day, he was in the mountains and in the tombs, crying out and cutting himself with stones.

The unclean spirit has greater power than humans because Satan is a fallen angel; as a result, no one could bind him, not even with chains. He had often been bound with shackles and chains. And when the chains had been pulled apart by him and the shackles broken in pieces, no one could tame him.

The unclean spirits are invisible beings. They do not have bodies of their own; thus, they cannot operate on their own. They are, therefore, looking for human bodies. They operate through human beings by either fully possessing or partially possessing them, depending upon the access to them. In this man, there were legions of many demons taking over his body, soul, and mind. People sometimes may not even be aware that the unclean spirits have possessed them and are operating in them and through them.

THE POWER OF THE INVISIBLE FORCES

Mark 1:23–26 says,

> And there was in their synagogue a man with an unclean spirit and he cried out, saying let us alone what have we to do with thee, thou Jesus of Nazareth? Art thou come to destroy us? I know thee who thou art' the Holy One of God. And Jesus rebuked him, saying, hold thy peace, and come out of him. And when the unclean spirit had torn him, and cried with a loud voice, he came out of him.

The demons and unclean spirits are subject to Jesus. They may harass, hurt, and possess humans; but they are afraid of the Holy One, the Son of the most high God, Jesus. He has given us the power of attorney to use His name. To that name of Jesus, Satan and his demons and unclean spirits tremble and bow. Matthew 12:22 says, "Then one was brought to Him who was demon-possessed, blind and mute, and He healed him, so that the blind and mute man both spoke and saw."

– 4 –

The Human Spirit

> And the LORD God formed man of the dust of the ground, and breathed into his nostrils the breath of life: and man became a living soul. (Gen. 2:7)

GOD CREATED HUMAN BEING out of dust and breathed life on them. We can therefore say human beings became the first spirit beings. The breath the human being is breathing is from God. God created human beings in His own image, and as a spirit being, He gave them the freedom to make their own choices.

God created Adam and Eve and placed them in the Garden of Eden and gave them dominion over the earth. He instructed them that they can eat and enjoy all the fruits of the trees, except the fruit of one tree, the one that gave knowledge of the good and evil. God loved them so much that He visited and communicated with them face to face.

Man is made out of dust, and God breathed into man's nostrils the breath of life. He breathed His very own divine breath into that body made out of clay. Therefore, man has the potential for a dual relationship with God. Through his spirit, which came from God, man relates to God. But through his body, which came from the earth, man relates to the world.

Genesis 2:16–17 says, "And the LORD God commanded the man saying, of every tree of the garden thou mayest freely eat. But of the tree of the knowledge of good and evil, thou shalt not eat of it for in the day that thou eatest thereof thou shalt surely die."

The day Adam and Eve disobeyed God, their spirit man died and they were separated from fellowship with God. From then on, everyone came into this world, born with a dead spirit and born as sinners. When we are born again, that is when we repent of our sin and surrender our life to the Lordship of Jesus. We are redeemed from sin, and our spirit man is born into the Spirit of God.

John 1:12 states this:

> But as many as received Him, to them gave he power to become the sons of God, even to them that believe on his name. Which were born, not of blood, nor of the will of the flesh, nor of the will of man, but of God.

All our sins are washed away by the blood of Jesus Christ. Our relationship with God is restored through Jesus Christ, who paid the penalty on our behalf. Our spirit man is made alive. Our spirits are reborn, but our souls (mind, will, and emotions) are not. Although we have no desire to sin or displease God anymore, our minds (conscious and subconscious) have been programmed to think, speak, and act like the world and the enemy. So we must renew our minds with God's Word to reap the full benefits of our salvation, think and act like the children of God, and receive our inheritance as His joint-heir.

Romans 12:1–2 says,

> I beseech therefore, brethren, by the mercies of God, that ye present your bodies a living sacrifice, holy, acceptable unto God, which is your reasonable service. And be not conformed to this world but be ye transformed by the renewing of your mind, that ye may prove what is that good, and acceptable, and perfect will of God.

We are to read, study, meditate, and live according to the Word of God. On a daily basis, we must allow the Word of God to change our mind and to conform to the image of God.

– 5 –

The Image of God

GENESIS 1:27 SAYS, "So God created man in His own image, in the image of God created He him; male and female created He them."

Man is created in the image of God. Lucifer and the one-third fallen angels cast down from heaven could not wage war against God, but Satan can make war against the very image of God within man. The devil is all out to defile that image, to destroy it, to humiliate it, and to kill it (John 10:10).

The Word in Genesis 3:1–5 reminds us,

> Now the serpent was more subtle than any beast of the field which the Lord God had made. And he said unto the woman. Yea, hath God said, Ye shall not eat of every tree of the garden? And the woman said unto the serpent we may eat of the fruit of the trees of the garden. But of the fruit of the tree which is in the midst of the garden God hath said, Ye shall not eat of it, neither shall ye touch it, lest ye die. And the serpent said unto the woman, Ye shall not surely die. For God doth know that in the day Ye eat thereof, then your eyes shall be opened, and Ye shall be as gods knowing good and evil.

Satan disguised himself as a serpent and tempted Adam and Eve into disobedience and rebellion. Satan questioned and discredited

God's word to Adam and Eve. The very next thing the serpent what tried to do was offer to Adam and Eve to eat of the fruit, saying, the fruit—which God said not to eat—will open their eyes and they will be like God, knowing good and evil. In other words, he suggested to them that they don't have to do what God said them to do, that they can be independent and be like God.

Lucifer rebelled against God, and he then instigated Adam and Eve to disobey God. Because Adam and Eve disobeyed God, they came under the control of Satan. Adam and Eve lost the dominion, power, and authority given to them. Satan deceived Adam and Eve and stole what belonged to Adam and Eve and became the god of the system of this world.

– 6 –

God Created Human Beings as a Triune Being

Humans are made of body, soul, and spirit. We cannot see the spirit being from our physical eyes. The human spirit can be controlled either by the Spirit of God or by the demonic spirit, depending to whom one submitted his or her will.

The Word in 1 Thessalonians 5:23 says, "And the very God of peace sanctify you wholly; and I pray God your whole spirit and soul and body be preserved blameless unto the coming of our Lord Jesus Christ."

– 7 –

The Kingdom of God

> From that time Jesus began to preach, and to say, Repent for the kingdom of heaven is at hand. And as Ye go, preach, saying, the kingdom of heaven is at hand. (Matt. 4:17; 10:7)

GOD CREATED ADAM AND Eve and gave the power and authority over the earth, but Satan disguised himself as a serpent and deceived them. Because they obeyed Satan, they came under the power of Satan. Jesus, God Himself, came as a man; defeated Satan, nailing his power into the cross; and took back the key stolen from Adam and Eve and established the kingdom of God on earth. Thus Jesus rescued the mankind from the prison door of Satan and restored the relationship with the Father God and gave them the key to the kingdom of God.

We read in the Word,

> And Jesus went about all Galilee, teaching in their synagogues, and preaching the gospel of the kingdom, and healing all manner of sickness and all manner of disease among the people. And Jesus went about all the cities and villages, teaching in their synagogues, and preaching the gospel of the kingdom, and healing every sickness and every disease among the people. (Matt. 4:23; 9:35)

THE POWER OF THE INVISIBLE FORCES

Satan afflicted people with sicknesses and diseases; whereas, Jesus came into the world and healed the sick and taught and preached the good news of the kingdom of God. In the kingdom of God, there is no sickness, misery, and heartache. Jesus came as a man and defeated the devil, Satan, and took the key and gave it to mankind.

As a man, Jesus left behind his deity status, and Satan attempted to tempt Jesus. But Satan could not succeed. God is a just God; He could not go back from His Word. So Jesus came as a human being with no sin and was born not of human relationship but of pure blood and destroyed the works of Satan. Jesus defeated and destroyed the works of the devil. We read these verses in the Holy Word of God:

> And I will give unto thee the keys of the kingdom of heaven and whatsoever thou shalt bind on earth shall be bound in heaven and whatsoever thou shalt loose on earth shall be loosed in heaven. (Matt. 16:19)

> That at the name of Jesus every knee should bow, of things in heaven, and things in earth, and things under the earth. And that every tongue should confess that Jesus Christ is Lord, to the glory of God the Father. (Phil. 2:10–11)

Jesus not only defeated Satan, but He took back from Satan the key which was stolen from Adam and Eve. He then gave the key to the followers of Christ and declared victory over Satan. We need not to be afraid of Satan anymore. Jesus gave us the power and authority over Satan and gave us the power of attorney to use His Name. Satan trembles at the Name of Jesus Christ of Nazareth.

Ephesians 1:20–23 tells us,

> Which He wrought in Christ when raised Him from the dead, and set him at his own right hand in the heavenly places. Far above all principality, power, and might, and dominion, and

> every name that is named, not only in this world, but also in that which is to come. And hath put all things under his feet, and gave him to be the head over all things to the church, which is his body, the fullness of him that filleth all in all.

God put all the power of Satan—his principality, his being the prince of the power of the air and the god of this world, and the demons—under the feet of Jesus. God made Jesus as the head of the church and gave the power and authority to the church over Satan. Jesus is our head, and we are His body. He put all things pertaining to Satan under our feet. Ephesians 3:17 says, "That Christ may dwell in your hearts by faith; that Ye being rooted and grounded in love."

Through Jesus Christ, God made a way to dwell in the hearts of those who surrendered their lives to the Lordship of Jesus. We read this in the Book of Colossians:

> Who hath delivered us from the power of darkness and hath translated us into the kingdom of His dear Son. (Col. 1:13)

> And you, being dead in your sins and the uncircumcision of your flesh, hath he quickened together with him, having forgiven you all trespasses; blotting out the handwriting of ordinances that was against us, which was contrary to us, and took it out of the way, nailing it to his cross; and having spoiled principalities and powers, he made a show of them openly, triumphing over them in it. (Col. 2:13–15)

No matter what our past life was, once we repent and ask for forgiveness from the Lord and make Him the Lord of our lives, He is just and faithful to cleanse us through His very own precious blood. His blood still has the power through the shed blood on the cross where He defeated Satan and rose again on the third day. He is the

Son of the Living God and made those who committed their lives to Him to be the children of God.

John 1:12 says, "But as many as received Him, to them gave He power to become the sons of God, even to them that believe on His Name."

– 8 –

The Redemption Plan of God

God created Adam and Eve, mankind, in His image with no sin. But Satan deceived Adam and Eve and caused them to disobey God. They then became sinners and guilty before the Holy God. Because of His love, God made a plan to redeem mankind from the prison door of Satan.

We read in Genesis 3:15, "And I will put enmity between thee and the woman, and between thy seed and her seed; it shall bruise thy head, and thou shalt bruise his heel." And in Genesis 3:21, we read, "Unto Adam also and to his wife did the Lord God make coats of skins, and clothed them."

God spoke through the prophet Isaiah regarding the birth of Christ in the Old Testament. It has been fulfilled in the New Testament. We read this in the Bible:

> For unto us a child is born, unto us a son is given: and the government shall be upon His shoulder: and his name shall be called Wonderful, Counsellor. The mighty God. The everlasting Father, The Prince of Peace. (Isa. 9:6)

The Book of Matthew also says this:

> Now the birth of Jesus Christ was on this wise: When as his mother Mary was espoused to Joseph, before they came together, she was found

> with child of the Holy Ghost. Then Joseph her husband, being a just man, and not willing to make her a public example, was minded to put her away privily. But while he thought on these things, behold, the angel of the Lord appeared unto him in a dream, saying, Joseph, The son of David, fear not to take unto thee Mary thy wife for that which is conceived in her is of the Holy Ghost. And she shall bring forth a son, and thou shalt call his name JESUS: for he shall save his people from their sins. (Matt. 1:18–21)

God used a human body—that is, a young woman called Mary—to come into this world as a human being with pure blood. Mary was conceived, not according to flesh but by the Holy Spirit. Until Jesus was born, Mary had no sexual relationship with Joseph. Although Mary was betrothed to Joseph, they did not come together. So when Joseph came to know Mary was pregnant, he was making a plan to put her out. But God intervened and sent His angel and told Joseph in a dream that conceived in Mary's womb is of the Holy Ghost, that it is going to be a son, and that he should name him as Jesus. The angel informed Joseph that God shall save His people from their sins.

We read in the Book of Matthew,

> And when they were departed, behold the Angel of the Lord appeareth to Joseph in a dream, saying, arise, and take the young child and his mother, and flee into Egypt, and be thou there until I bring thee word for Herod will seek the young child to destroy him. When he arose, he took the young child and his mother by night, and departed into Egypt. And was there until the death of Herod that it might be fulfilled which was spoken of the Lord by the prophet, saying, out of Egypt have I called my son. But when

> Herod was dead, behold an angel of the Lord appeareth in a dream to Joseph in Egypt. Saying, arise and take the young child and his mother and go into land of Israel for they are dead which sought the young child's life. And he arose, and took the young child and his mother and came into the land of Israel. (Matt. 2:13–15, 19–21)

Satan tried to kill the child conceived by the Holy Spirit through King Herod. But God escaped and rescued the child. God sent an angel and spoke with Joseph in a dream and instructed him to take the child and the mother to Egypt. Then when King Herod died, the angel appeared to Joseph in a dream and instructed him to take the mother and the child back to the land of Israel. While Satan tried to kill the child, he could not succeed. The Word of God speaks of this story:

> Then was Jesus was led up of the spirit into the wilderness to by trampled of the devil. And when he had fasted forty days and forty nights, he was afterward hungered. And when the tempter came to him, he said, if thou be the Son of God, command that these stones be made bread. But he answered and said, it is written, man shall not live by bread alone, but by every word that proceedeth out of the mouth of God. Then the devil taketh him up into the holy city, and setteeth him on a pinnacle of the temple. And saith unto him, if thou be the Son of God, cast thyself down for it is written, He shall give his angels charge concerning thee and in their hands they shall bear thee up, lest at any time thou dash thy foot against a stone. Jesus said unto him, it is written again, thou shall not tempt the Lord thy God. Again, the devil taketh him up into an exceeding high mountain and sheweth him all the. Kingdoms of

the world, and the glory of them. And saith unto him, all these things will I give thee, if thou wilt fall down and worship me. Then saith Jesus unto him, get thee hence, Satan for it is written, thou shalt worship the Lord thy God, and him only shalt thou serve. (Matt. 4:1–10)

Satan tempted Jesus on the lust of the flesh, the lust of the eyes, and the pride of life. But he could not succeed. Jesus defeated him by quoting the Scriptures:

> Forasmuch then as the children are partakers of flesh and blood, He also noted Himself likewise took part of the same, that through death He might destroy him that had the power of death, that is, the devil, and deliver them who through fear of death were all their lifetime subject to bondage. (Heb. 2:14–15)

Jesus was nailed to the cross by the power of Satan and laid down His life, shedding every drop of His blood, and rose again on the third day. Jesus conquered death and rescued mankind from the fear of death. He died and rose again so that mankind can have an eternal life through Jesus Christ.

– 9 –

The Power and Supremacy of God

> They hired Balaam against them to curse them, but our God turned the curse into a blessing. (Neh. 13:2)

THE AMMONITES AND THE Moabites hired Balaam to curse the follower of the God of the universe. Satan is the destroyer, but the Living God protects those who obey Him. We read this in the Word:

> Thou shalt have no other gods before Me. Thou shalt not make unto thee any graven image, or any likeness of any thing that is in heaven above or that is in the earth beneath, or that is in the water under the earth. Thou shalt not bow down thyself them, nor serve them for I the LORD thy God am a jealous God, visiting the iniquity of the father's upon the children unto the third and fourth generation of them that hate me. And shewing mercy unto thousands of them that love me, and keep my commandments. (Exod. 20:3–6)

The Living God instructed to everyone on the face of this earth through His Word to honor and worship Him alone. The wrath of

God will come upon those who do not worship Him until the third and fourth generations; whereas, His blessings will come upon those who worship and honor Him for thousands of generation. Matthew 28:18 says, "And Jesus came and spake unto them, saying, All power is given unto Me in heaven and in earth."

After Jesus rose again from death, He appeared to His disciples and declared to them that He has all the power in heaven and in earth. Satan had deceived Adam and Eve and robbed the power and authority given to Adam and Eve. John 5:26–27 says, "For as the Father has life in Himself, so He has granted the Son to have life in Himself, and has given Him authority to execute judgement also, because He is the Son of Man."

Jesus is the Son of God, and at the same time, He is the Son of Man. God is a just God. He had given to Adam and Eve to rule and reign and dominion over the earth. But Satan deceived Adam and Eve and became the god of the system of this world. Therefore, Jesus came into this world as a human and defeated Satan as a human and took back what he stole from Adam and Eve and gave that key for us who believes in Him. Jesus restored what had been stolen.

The Book of Mark relates this in these versus:

> And they were all amazed, insomuch that they questioned among themselves saying, what thing is this? What new doctrine is this? For with authority commandeth he even the unclean spirits and they do obey him. (Mark 1:27)

> And unclean spirits, when they saw Him, fell down before him, and cried, saying, Thou art the Son of God. (Mark 3:11)

Unclean spirits afflicted human beings and made the person to lose his mind, and people could not tame him. Yet when that same unclean spirit saw Jesus, he fell down before Him. They know that

He is Son of God the Creator. They are afraid of Him, which we can read in these verses:

> For this purpose the Son of God was manifested, that He might destroy the works of the devil. (1 John 3:8)

> Now is the judgment of this world now shall the Prince of this world be cast out. (John 12:31)

God has not given Satan the power and authority to exercise dominion over this earth. It does not belong to him, but he took it thru deception. The moment Jesus rose from the dead, Satan was cast out. This does not mean he was cast out of this world, or that he no longer is at work on earth. When he was cast out, his power over men was broken. He no longer has control over men. All those who believe in Jesus Christ and accept Him as their Lord and Savior are delivered out from under Satan's power and dominion of darkness and become part of the Kingdom of God (Colossians 1:13).

As "prince of this world," Satan is a ruler and exercise power and dominion only over the unsaved ones, who are in this world and the evil world system he has organized.

John 16:33, "I have conquered the world."

John 17:2, "You gave Him authority over all flesh."

Jesus conquered the world thru His shed Blood. He had committed no sin and He died so that we can live. He allowed the sinners to beat on Him, spit on Him and scourged Him. He did the finished work so that we can be made well.

Colossians 2:9, 15, "In Him, who is the head of all principality and power. Having disarmed principalities and powers, He (Jesus) made a public spectacle of them, triumphing over them in it."

THE POWER OF THE INVISIBLE FORCES

Jesus disarmed the principalities and powers of Satan. He stripped them out of all their weapons.

Ephesians 1:20-22, "Which he wrought in Christ, when he raised him from the dead and set him at his own right hand in the heavenly places. Far above all principality, and power, and might, and dominion, and every name that is named, not only in this world, but also in that which is to come. And hath put all things under his feet, and gave him to be the head over all things to the church."

God put all the power of darkness under the feet of Jesus and all the power of darkness bow to the Name of Jesus. Jesus has given the supreme power over all the power of the enemy. He is the head of the church and we the believers being the body of Christ all the power of the darkness are put under our feet. We need to know this truth and exercise the authority and power given to us.

– 10 –

The Holy Spirit

(M<small>ARK</small> 5:6-8) W<small>HEN HE</small> (demon—who possessed the man), saw Jesus from afar, he ran and worshiped Him. And he cried out with a loud voice and said, 'What have I to do with You Jesus, Son of the Most High God? I implore You by God that You do not torment me.'. (It was demon spirit was speaking to Jesus using that man's voice).

For He (Jesus), said to him (the unclean spirit), 'Come out of the man, unclean spirit.'

Jesus is holy and the unclean spirits are subject to the holy One. Jesus is full of the Holy Spirit. The Holy Spirit has the power and authority over unclean spirits. It is like the light and darkness. Jesus is of the Holy Spirit is the light and the unclean spirits have no light in them but darkness and full of evil.

Acts 1:8, "But ye shall receive power, after that the Holy Ghost is come upon you: and ye shall be witnesses unto me both in Jerusalem, and in all Judea, and in Samaria, and unto the uttermost part of the earth."

God blessed the followers of Christ to be filled with the infilling of the Holy Spirit. Thus those who have been filled with the Holy Spirit have the power over the demonic spirits to cast them out of the people who have been oppressed or possessed by the demonic spirits.

– 11 –

Jesus Taught on the Existence of Demons and Cast Them Out of People

A WOMAN OF CANAAN, HER daughter was grievously vexed with a devil. She cried out to Jesus saying, "have mercy on me, O Lord, son of David, my daughter is grievously vexed with a devil." The disciples tried to send her away. Jesus mentioned that he was sent to the lost sheep of Israel. Then she came and worshipped him saying, "Lord, help me." But Jesus answered, "it is not meet to take the children's bread, and to cast it to dogs." And she said "Truth, Lord, yet the dogs eat of the crumbs which fall from their masters table." Then Jesus answered and said unto her, "O woman, great is thy faith be it unto thee even as thou wilt." And her daughter was made whole from that very hour. (Matthew 15:22-28)

There was a man in their synagogue with an unclean spirit. Jesus rebuked and commanded that unclean spirit to come out of him. That unclean spirit had torn him, cried out with a loud voice and came out of him. (Mark 1:23-25, 32:34)

Even today there are people with an unclean spirit are sitting in the churches. Some of them are not even aware of it and the church leaders have no power to cast them out.

Mark 3:11, "And unclean spirits, when they saw him, fell down before him, and cried, saying, Thou art the Son of God."

The unclean spirits tormented and made human being lose his mind. That demon possessed man had no control over his own mind. The unclean spirits made him to live in the tombs and no one could go near him or tame him. He was like an insane crying, and cutting himself. He had so much power that even if he was bound by chains he would plucked those chains. But when they saw Jesus, they fell down before Him and cried with a loud voice and said what have I to do with thee Jesus, thou Son of the most high God? I adjure thee by God, that thou torment me not. They knew who Jesus was. They are subject to Jesus. They have no power before Jesus. They are afraid of Jesus. (Mark 3:11, Mark 5:2-13, 15, 18-20, Mark 9:17-29, Luke 8:27-33, Luke 9:42)

– 12 –

Unseen Supernatural Powers Given to the Followers of Jesus Christ

Mark 16:17, "And these signs shall follow them that believe, in my name shall they cast out Devils."

Mark 6:7, 13, "And He called unto Him the twelve, and began to send them forth by two and two; and gave them power over unclean spirits. And they cast out many Devils, and anointed with oil many that were sick, and healed the most."

The disciples after they received the power from Jesus over unclean spirits, they first preached that people should REPENT, then the disciples cast out many demons.
After that the disciples anointed with oil many who were sick and healed them.

Acts 5:16, "There came also a multitude out of the cities round about unto Jerusalem, bringing sick folks, and then which were vexed with unclean spirits and they were healed every one."

Acts 16:16-18, "And it came to pass, we went to prayer, a certain damsel possessed with a spirit of divination met us, which brought her masters much gain by soothsaying. The same followed Paul and us, and cried saying, these men are the servants of the most high God, which shew unto us the way of salvation. And this did she many days. But Paul, being grieved, turned and said to the spirit, I command thee in the name of Jesus Christ to come out of her. And he came out the same hour."

God has given His children—the followers of Christ, power and authority over Satan and all his evil forces through the Holy Spirit.

Luke 10:19, "Behold I give unto you power to tread on serpents and scorpions, and over all the power of the enemy, and nothing shall my any means hurt you."

Jesus is referring here to the power of Satan and of demons as serpents and scorpions. He has given us the power and authority over the power of the enemy. He has given us the power of attorney to use His Name. To the Name of Jesus every tongue has to confess that He is the Lord and every knee has to bow to that Name.

- 13 -

Demonic Spirits

Both the Old and New Testaments mention about demonic spirits operating in this world. Demonic spirits can inhabit in a human body. They desire to be in a human's or animal's body. They can cause a person to have superhuman physical strength. They can talk back and resist being cast out. Demons have intelligence. There are many names in God's Word identifying evil spirits. The Book of Acts read,

> Then certain of the vagabond Jews, exorcists, took upon them to call over them which had evil spirits the name of the Lord Jesus, saying, we adjure you by Jesus whom Paul preacheth. And there were seven sons of one Seeva, a Jew, and chief of the priests, which did so. And the evil spirit answered and said, Jesus I know, and Paul I know, but who are ye? And the man in whom the evil spirit was leaped on them, and overcame them, and prevailed against them, so that they fled out of that house naked and wounded. (Acts 19:13–16)

Jesus and Paul cast the demon out of people by the power of the Holy Spirit. Jesus gave His disciples His name, and His name has the power and authority to cast the demons out of people. Here, we see the vagabond Jews tried to cast the demon out. So the demons, instead of coming out, they leaped on them and overcame on them, so much so they fled out of that house, naked and wounded.

One must be filled with the Holy Spirit and must stand right with God in order to cast the demons out. The demons and the evil spirits will obey those who are walking in obedience to the word of God. Those who walk in obedience to the word of God, when they take up the name of Jesus with the power of the Holy Spirit, the demons will tremble and bow.

Blind Spirit

Matthew 12:22 reads, "Then was brought unto him one possessed with a devil, blind, and dumb, and he healed him, insomuch that the blind and dumb both spake and saw." The devil caused this man to be blind and dumb. So Jesus cast that demon out of him, and the man was able to see and talk.

Deaf and Dumb Spirit

Revelation 16:14 reads this:

> For they are the spirits of devils, working miracles, which go forth unto the kings of the earth and of the whole earth and of the whole world, to gather them to the battle of that great day of God Almighty.

It is important to know that there are spirits of the devil and there is a Spirit of God operating in this world. The Spirit of God would operate through those who surrender their lives to the Lordship of Jesus. The spirits of the devil would operate through those who would not surrender their lives to the Lordship of Jesus.

Seducing Spirit

Second Chronicles 33:9 reads, "So Manasseh made Judah and the inhabitants of Jerusalem to err, and to do worse than the heathen, whom the Lord had destroyed before the children of Israel."

In this chapter, King Manasseh seduced Judah and the inhabitants of Jerusalem to do more evil than the nations whom the Lord had destroyed before the children of Israel. When he was afflicted by God for his evil deeds, he repented and turned to God and commanded Judah to serve the God of Israel. He then removed, destroyed, and cast out all foreign gods, idols, and images. He repaired the altar of the Lord and commanded Judah to serve the Lord God of Israel.

We have to examine and see if there is any open door to the Satan in our lives. Are there any idols or altars built for foreign gods in our hearts that need to be demolished, destroyed, or to be cast out? Remember, any action or deed contrary to the Word of God will open the door to Satan. God should be first in our lives. Idol worship is not just the images; it can be our job, our ministry, our family, our money, our business, sports, and intellectual who take the place of God are considered as idols.

Proverbs 7:21–23 reads this:

> With her enticing speech she caused him to yield, with her flattering lips she SEDUCED him. Immediately he went after her, as an ox goes to the slaughter, or as a fool to the correction of the stocks. Till an *arrow struck his liver*, as a bird hastens to the snare, he did not know it would cost his life.

The phrase "arrow struck his liver" can be equated to hepatitis C. The spirit of seduction will cause one to sin, which ultimately destroy one's life. It is the strategy of the enemy to destroy the lives. We read in 1 Timothy 4:1, "Now the Spirit speaketh expressly that in the latter times some shall depart from the faith giving heed to seducing spirits, and doctrines of devils."

Angel of Light

The Bible in 2 Corinthians 11:13–14 reads, "For such are false apostles, deceitful workers, transforming themselves into apostles of Christ. And no wonder! For Satan himself transforms himself into an angel of light."

Jealous Spirit

Take note of Numbers 5:29–31:

> This is the law of jealousies, when a wife goeth aside to another of her husband, and is defiled: Or when the spirit of jealousy cometh upon him, and he be jealous over his wife, and shall set the woman before the Lord, and the priest shall execute upon her all this law. Then shall the man be guiltless from iniquity, and this woman shall bear her iniquity.

Cunning Spirit

The Word also reminds us to be diligent in the face of the cunning spirit: "Now the serpent was more subtle than any beast of the field which The Lord God had made" (Gen. 3:1, 4–5).

Familiar Spirit

The familiar spirit is also discussed in the Book of Leviticus:

> And the soul that turneth after such as have familiar spirits, and after wizards, to go a whoring after them, I will even set my face against that soul, and will cut him off from among his people. A man also or woman that hath a familiar spirit, or that is a wizard, shall surely be put to death;

they shall stone them with stones: their blood shall be upon them. (Lev. 20:6, 27)

Lying Spirit

The Word reminds us in Genesis 3:4–5,

> And he said unto the woman, Yea, hath God said, Ye shall not eat of every tree of the garden? And the serpent said unto the woman, Ye shall not surely die: For God doth know that in the day we eat thereof, then your eyes shall be opened, and Ye shall be as gods, knowing good and evil.

The serpent told a lie to the woman, Eve. Surely, she did not die physically but she died spiritually, and the separation from God and mankind took place the moment Eve heeded the voice of the serpent and disobeyed the voice of God.

We also learn this in the Word:

> And he said, I will go out and be a lying spirit in the mouth of all his prophets. And the Lord said, thou shall entice him, and thou shall also prevail, go out and do even so. Now therefore, behold, The Lord hath put a lying spirit in the mouth of these thy prophets, and the Lord hath spoken evil against thee. (2 Chron. 18:21–22)

> Ye are of your father the devil, and the lusts of your father Ye will do. He was a murderer from the beginning, and abode not in the truth, because there is no truth in him. When he speaketh a lie, he speaketh of his own: for he is a liar and the father of it. He that is of God hearth

God's words: Ye therefore hear them not, because
Ye are not of God. (John 8:44, 47)

Remember, Satan is the source of all lies. He hates truth. One of his strategies is to distort the truth. It is the truth that sets the mankind free out of Satan's bondage. Satan binds the hearts and minds of unbelievers so they will be unable to see the truth.

Spirit of the Philistines and the Arabs

The Second Book of Chronicles reads this:

> Moreover the Lord stirred up against Jehoram the spirit of the Philistines and the Arabians, that were near the Ethiopians. And they came up into Judah, and brake into it, and carried away all the substance that was found in the king's house, and his sons also, and his wives, so that there was never a son left to him, save Jehoahaz, the youngest of his sons. And after all this the Lord smote him in his bowels with an incurable disease. (2 Chron. 21:16–18)

Debased Mind

We learn of this in the Word in Romans 1:26–32:

> For this reason God gave them up unto vile affections: for even their women exchanged did change the natural use into that which is against nature. And likewise also the men, leaving the natural use of the women, burned in their lust one toward another men with men working that which is unseemly, and receiving in themselves that recompence of their error which was meet. And even as they did not like to retain God in

their knowledge, God gave them over to a reprobate mind, to do those things which are not convenient. Being filled with all unrighteousness, fornication, wickedness, covetousness, maliciousness, full of envy, murder, debate, deceit, malignity, whisperers, back biters, haters of God, despitefully, proud, boasters, inventors of evil things, disobedient to parents. Without understanding covenant breakers, without natural affection, implacable, unmerciful. Who knowing the judgment of God, that they which commit such things are worthy of death, not only do the same, but have pleasure in them that do them.

Characteristics of the Spirit of Ahab

In disobedience to God, King Ahab married princess Jezebel, the daughter of Ethabaal, king of the Sidonians. She was not from the tribes of Israel.

The spirit of Ahab is weak, childish, unreliable, a brat, a pouter, carelessness, foolishness, insecurity, indecision, lack of character, subject to temper tantrums, relinquishes authority, has a wrong concept of his authority, lust, masturbation, a perverse spirit, lazy, fearful of rebuke, fearful of responsibility, has a lustful fantasy, undependable, fearful of failing, blameful of others (mainly, the wife), only justifying himself, leans on his wife, is a mama's boy, has relinquished the spiritual authority over his house, and is irresponsible (2 Chron. 18:1–3, 33 ; 21:4–6 ; 22:2–4, 6–7).

Characteristics of the Spirit of Jezebel

Jezebel introduced the worship of Baal into Israel. She brought 450 prophets of Baal and 400 prophets of Ashera to the palace, where they ate at the table (1 Kings 16:29–33; 21:1–4, 7, 16, 19–25, 28–29; 2 Kings 9:6–10, 22, 30–35).

The spirit of Jezebel is pride; arrogance; domination; scheming; superiority; center of attention; gossip; argument; strife; witchcraft; antisubmissiveness; stubbornness; resistance; an "I am better than you" attitude; a "what I say is the way it is" attitude; an "I know better, my choices are the best, I know better" attitude; competitive; authoritarian; a "do it my way" attitude; selfishness; ego; lust; pornography; masturbation; haughtiness; jealousy; control; manipulation; rebellion; selfish; self-centeredness; self-righteousness; self-seeking; taker and not giver; inconsiderate; narcissistic; deception; argumentative; revenge; mind control; critical spirit; judgmental; accusing; fault finding; suspicion; greed; discontentment; disobedience; headstrong; intimidating; strife; disagreement; quarreling; fighting; dispute; insist; destruction; hatred; contentious; matrimonial discord; never satisfied; physical abuse, mental abuse, emotional abuse, psychological abuse, and verbal abuse; and humiliation of sons or daughters.

Command the Jezebel spirit to come out of that person. That demon might talk to you and might even threaten you. Remind that person that your authority comes from the third heaven—at the right hand of the Father, in Jesus Christ. That demon might say, "That person is mine," or something similar. Remind that demon that person belongs to the Lord Jesus Christ. Remind Jezebel that her "empire" is destroyed. Then ask the Lord to send the angels and to cast the Jezebel spirit out of that person.

Spirit of Fear

Genesis 3:10 reads, "So he [Adam] said, I heard Your voice in the garden, and I was afraid because I was naked and I hid myself."

Up until Adam and Eve disobeyed God, they did not know what the fear was like. The day they disobeyed God's Word and obeyed Satan, Satan brought on Adam and Eve and into the entire mankind all kinds of negative forces—sickness, diseases, and heartache—because he robbed the key given to Adam and Eve.

Spirit of Blame, Defensiveness, and Accusation

Genesis 3:12–13 reads, "The man said the woman whom You gave to be with me, she gave me of the tree and I ate. The woman said, the serpent deceived me, and I ate."

Adam and Eve never took the responsibility for their action but tried to blame and accuse the other.

Spirit of Deception

We are reminded of deception in Genesis 3:13: "The serpent deceived me." And in Revelation 20:2–3, we read this:

> And he laid hold on the dragon, that old serpent, which is the Devil, and Satan, and bound him a thousand years. And cast him into the bottomless pit and shut him up, and set a seal upon him, that he should deceive the nations no more, till the thousand years should be fulfilled and after that he must be loosed a little season.

Remember, deception is the strategy of Satan.

Spirit of Disobedience

We read this verse in the Word about disobedience:

> Now the serpent was more subtle than any other beast of the field which the Lord God had made. And He said unto the woman, Yea, hath God said, Ye shall not eat of every tree of the garden? And the woman said unto the serpent, we may eat of the fruit of the tree of the garden. But of the fruit of the tree which is in the midst of the garden, God hath said, Ye shall not eat of it, neither shall Ye touch it, lest Ye die. And the serpent

said unto the woman, Ye shall not surely die. For God doth know that in the day Ye eat thereof, then your eyes shall be opened, and Ye shall be as gods, knowing good and evil. And when the woman saw that the tree was good for food, and that it was pleasant to the eyes, and a tree to be desired to make one wise, she took of the fruit thereof, and did eat, and gave also unto her husband with her, and he did eat. (Gen. 3:1–6)

Satan attacked Eve's mind. Satan knew that God had commanded Adam and Eve not to eat of the tree of knowledge of good and evil, but Satan tried to plant doubt in Eve's mind. He wanted her to question God's word. He lied to Eve. He contradicted God's word. Satan told her that she would not die if she ate the forbidden fruit.

Eve not only listened to Satan, but also she carried on a conversation with him. Eve knew that God commanded them not to eat the fruit of the tree that gives knowledge of good and evil. She also knew that God had told them that if they eat that forbidden fruit, they would die. Instead of rejecting Satan's lies, she listened to him. She not only ate the fruit, but she also gave the fruit to her husband and he too ate it. As we knew, they did not die physically but died spiritually and the separation from God took place. Satan became the God of the system of this world and brought all kinds of misery and trouble to mankind.

Spirit of Shame

Genesis 3:7 speaks of the spirit of shame: "And the eyes of them both were opened, and they knew that they were naked: and they sewed fig leaves together, and made themselves aprons."

Spirit of Greed

Proverbs 28:25 teaches us of greed: "He that is of a proud heart stirreth up strife: but he that putteth his trust in the Lord shall be made fat."

Acts 5:1–10 reminds us this story of greed:

> But a certain man named Ananias, with Sapphira his wife, sold a possession. And kept back part of the price, his wife also being privy to it, and brought a certain part, and laid it at the apostles feel. But Peter said, Anannias, why hath Satan filled thine heart to lie to the a Holy Ghost, and to keep back part of the price of the land? Whiles it remained, was it not thine own? And after it was sold, was it not I'm thine own power? Why hast thou conceived this thing in thine heart? Thou hast not lied unto men, but unto God. And Anannias hearing these words fell down, and gave up the ghost and great fear came on all them that heard these things. And the young men arose, wound him up, and carried him out, and buried him. And it was about the space of three hours after, when his wife, not knowing what was done, came in. And Peyer answered unto her, tell me whether Ye sold the land for so much? And she said, yea, for so much. Then Peter said unto her, how is it that Ye have agreed together so tempt the Spirit of the Lord? Behold, my he feet of them which buried thy husband are at the door, and shall carry thee out. Then fell she down straightway at his feet, and yielded up the ghost: and the young men came in, and found her dead, and, carrying her forth buried her by her husband.

Spirit of Gluttony

Proverbs 28:7 says this of gluttony: "Whoso keepeth the law is a wise son: but he that is a companion of riotous [gluttons] men shameth his father."

Spirit of Independence

Genesis 3:7–8 teaches this about independence:

> Then the eyes of both of them were opened, and they knew that they were naked and they sewed fig leaves together and made themselves coverings. Adam and his wife hid themselves from the presence of The Lord God among the trees of the garden.

Spirit of Infirmity

The Word says this of the spirit of infirmity:

> And he was teaching in one of the synagogues on the sabbath. And, behold, there was a woman which had a spirit of infirmity eighteen years, and was bowed together, and could in no wise lift up herself. And when Jesus saw her, he called her to him, and said unto her, woman, thou art loosed from thine infirmity. And he laid his hands on her, and immediately she was made straight, and glorified God. And ought not this woman being a daughter of Abraham whom Satan hath bound these eighteen years, be loosed from this bond on the sabbath day? (Luke 13:10–13, 16)

Unclean Spirit

The New Testament has a lot to say about unclean spirits:

> When the unclean spirit is gone out of a man, he walketh through dry places, seeking rest, and findeth none. (Matt. 12:43)

> And there was in their synagogue a man with an unclean spirit; and he cried out, saying let us alone; what have we to do with thee, thou Jesus of Nazareth? Art thou come to destroy us? I know thee who thou art the Holy One of God. (Mark 1:23–24)

> For He said unto him, come out of the man, thou unclean spirit. And he asked him, what is thy name? And he answered, saying, my name is Legion: for we are many. (Mark 5:8–9)

> When Jesus saw that the people came running together, he rebuked the foul spirit, saying unto him, thou dumb and deaf spirit, I charge thee, come out of him, and enter no more into him. (Mark 9:25)

> And as he was yet a coming the devil threw him down, and Tate him. And Jesus rebuked the unclean spirit, and healed the child, and delivered him again to his father. (Luke 9:42)

> Because that, when they knew God, they glorified him not as God, neither were thankful: but became vain in their imaginations, and their foolish heart was darkened. Professing themselves to be wise, they became fools. And changed the

glory of the incorruptible God into an image made like to corruptible man, and to birds, and four footed beasts and creeping things. Wherefore God also gave them up to uncleanness through the lusts of their own hearts, to dishonor their own bodies between themselves. Who changed the truth of God into s lie, and worshipped and served the creature more than the Creator, who is blessed for ever. (Rom. 1:21–25)

Pride

Ezekiel 28:17–18 says this of pride:

> Your heart was lifted up because of your beauty; you corrupted your wisdom for the sake of your splendor. You defiled your sanctuaries by the multitude of your iniquities, by the iniquity of your trading.

God created Lucifer with musical ability, beauty, and wisdom. The physical beauty and the multitude of God-given possessions such as, beauty, wisdom, and music lifted his heart with pride. The pride produced iniquity in his heart. Lucifer was in charge of the worship and was responsible for the sanctuary of God in heaven, but pride entered his heart. Pride is the deadly sin. Pride had been the root of Lucifer's rebellion against God. As a result, he not only lost his position, his beauty, but also he was cast down from heaven from the presence of God; and one-third of the angels who followed him were cast down with him.

The Second Book of Chronicle says this:

> In those days Hezekiah was sick to the death and prayed unto the Lord and he spake unto him, and he gave him a sign. But Hezekeiah rendered not again according to the

> benefit done unto him; for his heart was lifted up therefore there was wrath upon him and upon Judah and Jerusalem. Notwithstanding Hezekiah humbled himself for the pride of his heart, both he and the inhabitants of Jerusalem, so that the wrath of the Lord came not upon them in the days of Hezekiah. And Hezekiah had exceeding much riches and honor; and he made himself treasuries for silver, and for gold, and for precious stones, and for spices, and for shields, and for all manner of pleasant jewels; storehouses also for the increase of corn, and wine, and oil; and stalls for all manner of beasts, and cotes for flocks. Moreover he provided him cities and possessions of flocks and herds in abundance for God had given his substance very much. This same Hezekiah also stopped the upper watercourse of Gihon, and brought it straight down to the west side of the city of David. And Hezekiah prospered in all his works. (2 Chron. 32:24–30)

King Hezekiah honored God and encouraged his people to seek after the living God. And when the enemy—Sennacherib, king of Assyria—boasted of his power, ridiculed the Lord God, and threatened to take over the city, King Hezekiah, along with the prophet Isiah, cried to God. God then sent an angel and protected Hezekiah and his people.

The Lord blessed Hezekiah and made Hezekiah and his people prosper immensely, but when he opened the door to the spirit of pride, the wrath of God came upon him and over Judah and Jerusalem. He then humbled himself—he and the inhabitants of Jerusalem—for the pride of his heart so that the wrath of the Lord did not come upon them in the days of Hezekiah. God blessed Hezekiah and prospered him in all his works.

The First Book of John 2:15–17 teaches this:

> Love not the world, neither the things that are in the world. If any man love the world, the love of the Father is not in him. For all that is in the world, the lust of the flesh and the lust of the eyes, and the pride of life, is not of the Father, but is of the world. And the world passeth away, and the lust thereof but he that doth the will of God abideth for ever. (1 John 2:15–17)

Apostle John warned believers to be aware of three deadly temptations: (1) the lust of the flesh, (2) the lust of the eyes, and (3) the pride of life. In the Garden of Eden, Satan tempted Eve with all these three and brought misery into her and Adam's life. Even today, he tempts the people into sin with pride of possession and pride of physical beauty.

Remember Proverbs 16:18: "Pride goeth before destruction, and an haughty spirit before a fall."

King Saul and Evil Spirits

We first learn of King Saul and the evil spirits in 1 Samuel 31:2–8:

> And the Philistines followed hard after Saul, band after his sons; and the Philistines slew Jonathan, and Abinadab, and Malchi-Shula, the sons of Saul.
>
> And the battle went sore against Saul, and the archers hit him, and he was wounded of the archers.
>
> Then said Saul to his armor bearer, Draw thy sword, and thrust me through there with; lest these uncircumcised come and abuse me. But his armourbearer would not; for he was sore afraid. So Saul took a sword, and fell upon it.

> And when his armourbearer saw that Saul was dead, he fell likewise on the sword, and died.
> So Saul died and three sons, and all his house died together.
> And when all the men of Israel that were in the valley saw that they fled, and that Saul and his sons were dead, then they forsook their cities, and fled: and the Philistines came and dwelt in them.
> And it came to pass on the morrow, when the Philistines came to strip the slain, that they found Saul and his sons fallen in mount Gilboa.

Saul disobeyed God. He was not faithful and did not keep the word of the Lord. Moreover, he consulted the medium for guidance rather than seeking the help from God. As a result, the door was open to the enemy to destroy Saul and his family. He and his three sons were killed simultaneously by the enemy. They cut his head off and fastened his head in the temple of the dragon. Saul was not protected by God because he put himself under Satan, who destroyed him. Through Saul, the enemy got an access to destroy his sons as well.

King David

In 1 Chronicle 21:1–27; 27:23–24, 34, Satan stood up against Israel and moved David to number Israel, which was not of God.

King David did not realize that suggestion was from Satan. God spoke to him through Joab, the general of the king's army, not do so, causing guilt in Israel. But King David did not heed Joab's warning. As a result, he came under the wrath of God because he heeded the voice of the enemy and displeased God. God gave David victory over their enemies, but now because David displeased God, God struck Israel. Because of David's sin, the whole nation came under judgement.

God had said that He would multiply Israel like the stars of the heaven; therefore, they were not supposed to take the census. Then King David admitted his mistake, repented, and asked for forgiveness from the Lord.

Eye

Luke 11:34–36 says this:

> The light of the body is the eye: therefore when thine eye is single, thy whole body also is full of light; but when thine eye is evil, thy body also is full of darkness. Take heed therefore that the light which is in thee be not darkness.

We read this in Matthew 6:22–24 as well:

> The light of the body is the eye: if therefore thine eye be single, thy whole body shall be full of light. But if thine eye be evil, thy whole body shall be full of darkness. If therefore the light that is in thee be darkness, how great is that darkness.

Pornography

Job 31:1 says, "I made a covenant with mine eye; why then should I think upon a maid?" In the present time, many are bound by pornography, including so-called Christians. It is like a nicotine—easy to get in but difficult to get out. It is the satanic forces behind these addictions; those addicted need the deliverance to set them free from that bondage.

Talebearers, Slanderers, Liars, and Flatterers

The Bible talks extensively about these kinds of people:

> He that goeth about as a tale bearer revealeth secrets; therefore meddle not associate with him that flattereth with his lips. (Prov. 20:19)

> They are all grievous revolvers, walking with slanders: they are brass and iron: they are all corrupters. (Jer. 6:28)

> Take ye heed every one of his neighbor, and trust ye not in any brother: for every brother will utterly supplant, and every neighbor will walk with slanders. And they will deceive every one his neighbour and will not speak the truth: they have taught their tongue to speak lies, and weary themselves to commit iniquity. Thine habitation is in the midst of deceit; through deceit they refuse to know me, saith the LORD. (Jer. 9:4–6)

> In thee are men that carry tales to shed blood: and in thee they eat upon the mountains: in midst of thee they commit lewdness. (Ezek. 22:9)

The talebearer and the flatterer are very closely related to each other. Flattery and lies are also related one another.

Disobedience to the Word of God and Our Conscience

We read this in the Word: "But if you have bitter envy and self-seeking in your hearts, do not boast and lie against the truth. This wisdom does not descend from above, but is earthly, sensual, demonic" (James 3:14–15). Disobedience to the Word of God is being operated through the demonic spirit.

Ephesians 2:2 says, "Wherein in time past ye walked according to the course of this world, according to the Prince of the power of the air, the spirit that now worketh in the children of disobedience." Anyone who is in rebellion against God is automatically under the authority of Satan. The enmity is of the devil. Those who have not submitted their lives to the Lordship of Jesus—the enemy works through their minds and they are not even aware of it. Once we commit our lives to the Lordship of Jesus, the power of Satan is broken off us because Jesus put to death the enmity.

The Bible speaks of this in the Book of Ephesians:

> And that he might reconcile both unto God in one body by the cross, having slain the enmity thereby. (Eph. 2:16)

> And He made alive, who were dead in trespasses and sins, in which you once walked according to the course of this world, according to the prince of the power of the air, the spirit who now works in the sons of disobedience, among whom also we all once conducted ourselves in the lusts of our flesh, fulfilling the desires of the flesh and of the mind, and we're by nature children of wrath, just as the others. that at that time you were without Christ, being aliens from the commonwealth of Israel and strangers from the covenants of promise, having no hope and without God in the world. (Eph. 2:1–3, 12)

Satan rules over those who are in rebellion against God. We were born with a disobedient nature. Everyone who descended from Adam has inherited the nature of a rebel. That nature makes us subject to Satan. This we learn from the Book of John:

> Jesus answered them, verily, verily, I say unto you, whosoever committeth sin is the servant of sin. Ye are of your father the devil, and the lusts of your father ye will do. He was a murderer from the beginning and abode not in the truth, because there is no truth in him. When he speaketh a lie, he speaketh of his own: for he is a liar and the father of it. (John 8:34, 44)

Those who has not given their lives to the Lordship of Jesus, no matter how good they are, they come under the influence of Satan, and Satan will instigate them to do the wrong things. Because it is the nature of Satan. Romans 8:7 says, "Because the carnal mind is enmity against God: for it is not subject to the law of God, neither indeed can be."

The carnal mind is enmity toward God. The carnal mind opens the door to Satan, and he does not want to abide by the law of God. Proverbs 3:31–32 says, "Envy thou not the oppressor, and choose none of his ways; for the froward is abomination to The Lord."

We read this in the First Book of John:

> He that saith he is in the light, and hateth his brother, is in darkness even until now. He that loveth his brother abideth in the light, and there is none occasion of stumbling in him. But he that hateth his brother is in darkness, and walketh in darkness and knowth not whither he goeth, because that darkness hath blinded his eyes. (1 John 2:9–11)

> In this the children of God are manifest, and the children of the devil: whosoever doeth not righteousness is not of God, neither he that loveth not his brother. We know that we have passed from death unto life, because we love the brethren. He that loveth not his brother abideth in death. Whosoever hateth his brother is a murderer: and ye know that no murderer hath eternal life abiding in him. (1 John 3:10, 14–15)

Love is of God, and the opposite of it hate is—of the devil. When we hate our brother or our fellow man or woman, we are operating in the influence of Satan. Jesus said that to whom we obey, we become their servant. Here, it is clear that whoever hates his brother or sister is a murderer and that he or she forfeit the eternal life: "Ye adulterers and adulteresses, know ye not that the friendship of the world is enmity with God? Whosoever therefore will be a friend of the world is the enemy of God" (James 4:4).

Remember, no one can love the world and at the same love God. Our first priority should be to God.

Unforgiveness

The Bible teaches of unforgiveness in these verses:

> You have heard that it was said by them of old time. Thou shall not kill; and whosoever shall kill shall be in danger of the judgement. But I say unto you, that whosoever is angry with his brother without a cause shall be in danger of the judgement and whosoever shall say to his brother, Raca, shall be in danger of the council: but whosoever shall say, thou fool, shall be in danger of hell fire. Therefore if thou bring thy gift to the altar, and there rememberest that thy brother hath ought against thee; leave there the gift before the altar, and go thy way; first be reconciled to thy brother, and then come and offer thy gift. Agree with thine adversary quickly, whiles thou art in the way with him; lest at any time the adversary deliver thee, to the judge, and the judge deliver thee to the officer and thou be cast into prison. Verily I say unto thee, thou shalt by no means come out thence till thou hast paid the uttermost farthing. (Matt. 5:21–26)

> For if ye forgive men their trespasses, your Heavenly Father will also forgive you: but if ye forgive not men their trespasses, neither will your Father forgive your trespasses. (Matt. 6:14–15)

Forgiveness is not an option—it is a must in order for us to be right with God. Unforgiveness hinders our own blessing from God. According to this, it is important for us to learn that how we treat others has a consequence.

Worry

We read this in Matthew 6:25–34:

> Therefore I say unto you, take no thought for your life, what ye shall eat, or what ye shall drink: nor yet for your body, what ye shall put on. Is not the life more than meat, and the body than raiment? Behold the fowls of the air for they sow not, neither do I they reap, nor gather into barns; yet your Heavenly Father feedeth them. Are ye not much better than they? Which of you by taking thought can add one cubit unto his stature? And why take ye thought for raiment? Consider the lilies of the field how they grow; they toil not, neither do they spin. And yet I say unto you, that even Solomon in all his glory was not arrayed like one of these. Wherefore, if God so clothe the grass of the field, which today is, and tomorrow is cast into the oven, shall be not much more clothe you, O ye of little faith? Therefore take no thought saying, what shall we eat? or what shall we drink? or, wherewithal shall we be clothed? (For after all these things do the Gentiles seek). for your Heavenly Father knoweth that ye have need of all these things. But seek ye first the kingdom of God, and his righteousness and all these things shall be added unto you. Take therefore no thought for the morrow: for the morrow shall take thought for the things of itself sufficient unto the day is the evil thereof.

Worry is what the enemy attacks people with, especially in pressure and stressful times. Jesus has commanded us to put aside worry. Jesus assures us that our Heavenly Father knows what we need even before we ask so there is no reason to worry. When we desire God's righteousness through Christ Jesus to be reflected in our words and actions, when we seek to be dedicated to His way over our own way, when we seek to execute His plan in place of our own plan, when our primary goal is for the fulfillment of His Kingdom within our hearts and lives—worry will cease to control us and God will be free to move to meet our every need. As you try to resist worry, the enemy will try to draw you back into old habit pattern of worry. It is up to you to decide and resist it in the name of Jesus. God has given you a free will and the power to resist by the power of the Holy Spirit.

Sexual Demons

The Word tells of this story in Matthew 5:27–32:

> Ye have heard that it was said by them of old time, thou shalt not commit adultery: but I say unto you, that whosoever looketh on a woman to lust after her hath committed adultery with her already in his heart. And if thy right eye offend thee, pluck it out, and cast it from thee: for it is profitable for thee that one of thy members should perish, and not that thy whole body should be cast into hell. And if thy right hand offend thee, cut it off, and cast it from thee: for it is profitable for thee that one of thy members should perish, and not that thy whole body should be cast into hell. It hath been said, whosoever shall put away his wife, let him give her a writing of divorcement: but I say unto you, that whosoever shall put away his wife, saving for the cause of fornication, causeth her to commit

> adultery: and whosoever shall marry her that is divorced committeth adultery.

Sexual sin destroys marriages and brings sadness, shame, and heartache. Moreover, sexual sin damages one's own body.

– 14 –

An Open Door to Unseen Evil Forces

God is love, and He created human beings to love and to be loved. He cares for His creation. But the enemy, the adversary of God—Satan—comes in whenever there is an open door and destroys human beings (John 10:10). It is not God who brings misery, pain, heartache, and death to human beings; however, its author is Satan. Some Christians are ignorant and think some sicknesses are to chastise them or to bring closer to God. God has given His people His word for everyone to follow and to come under His blessings and to live a victorious life. Whoever disobeys His word not only comes under His curse but also opens the door to Satan to come in and to destroy their lives. At times, some people might be ignorant, and they do it for fun. But that doesn't stop the enemy from coming in. Even if one is innocent or ignorant, that would not stop the enemy to invade the minds of the people and to destroy them (Lev. 18:4–5, 26, 30; 19:37; 26:1–39; Exod. 20:1–17, 23; Deuteronomy 5:7–21).

We see in Deuteronomy 5:9–10 that God visits the iniquity of the fathers upon the children to the third and fourth generations of those who hate Him. But God shows mercy to thousands of generations to those who love Him and keep His commandments. In other words, when one breaks God's commandments, it opens the door to Satan to come in and to destroy him or her. That is the reason why we see some of them be saved and love the Lord and do the right things, yet they still face problems in life. In such situations, we need to see if they are coming under the third and fourth generations of God's curse; if so, we can break that generational curse and have those people to be free from that generational curse. At the same time, we see some people live such smooth lives. Everything is going well in their life because they come under the blessing of a thousand generations.

Spiritism

Acts 19:18–19 says this:

> And many who had believed came confessing and telling their deeds. Also, many of those who had practiced magic brought their books together and burned them in the sight of all. And they counted up the value of them, and it totaled fifty thousand pieces of silver.

When people are involved in any kind of Spiritism—which is against the will, plan, and purpose of God—that will open the door to Satan to come in and to destroy them. God commanded not to practice divination or soothsaying. God also commanded not to regard mediums and familiar spirits and not to seek after those who would defile them. God also commanded not to be involved in telekinesis, subliminal techniques, remote influences, soul travel, astral projections, clairvoyance, channeling, psychic commands, psychic projection, black magic, witchcraft, martial arts and yoga, new-age thinking, alcohol, drugs, and any other form of mind control, which opens the door for Satan to come in. They can only be set-free through deliverance (Lev. 19:26, 31; 20:6, 27; Isa. 47:9–15).

Some Christians, including some churches, are being deceived. They would call it "Christian yoga," and it is for the wellness of the body. They may not realize that they may have opened a door for evil spirits, even Kundalini, to enter in. Yoga has been introduced successfully into schools, institutions, and in many walks of life in the Western countries, including United States. Yoga and the Kundalini spirit originate from the occult of eastern religion.

Sexual Sin

God commanded human beings to keep His commandments and to stay away from incest, not to mate with another in customary impurity, homosexuality, bestiality, prostitution, adultery, illegitimate births, etc. (Lev. 18:6–22; 19:29; 20:10–21; Deut. 23:2).

When someone fails to obey God's commandment and commits sexual sin, it not only damages one's own body but also causes the land and the nation to become defiled. A bastard shall not enter into the congregation of the Lord; even to his tenth generation, he shall he not enter into the congregation of the Lord. These all open the door for Satan to come in to destroy their lives (Lev. 18:24–25, 29; Deut. 23:2).

Tattoos

God commanded not to make any cuttings on our body or any marks on our body (Lev. 19:28). But when one does these, it opens the door for Satan to come in and bring all kinds of misery.

- 15 -

Jesus Is the Way

Repentance

Jesus said in John 14:6, "I am the way, the truth, and the life; no man cometh unto the Father, but by me."

Once the door opened to the enemy that is to Satan, it is difficult to close it. The only way one can be set-free from that bondage is by repenting of their sin, renouncing the Satanic action, and surrendering their lives to the Lordship of Jesus. Some time we need to find out where and when the door was opened to the enemy. Accordingly, we need to close the door opened to the enemy. Once the door is closed and accept Jesus as their Lord, He cleanses them and set them free once and for all from all unrighteousness. Then on, they need to know Him by reading the Word of God and obey His Word so that they can lead a victorious lives,(Leviticus 26:40-45.)

– 16 –

Personal Experiences

I WAS RAISED IN A denominational church where the teaching of the infilling of the Spirit was absent. My mother was healthy and strong, but all of a sudden, she became nonfunctional. The church where I belonged had the form of godliness with no power. I sought the medical help, but it was no use. I then tried to get help from eastern religion practitioners who said that my mother was suffering because someone did witchcraft on her for her to die within six months. That curse was so dangerous that they could not break or remove it. Sure enough, my mother died in six months' time.

My mother's death caused me to lose hope and trust in Jesus Christ. I became an atheist. I could not overcome the grief and sorrow of the loss of my mother. On the third year, my grief and sorrow turned into fear. I could not concentrate or sleep, and I was tormented by the fear of death. I then cried out and prayed to an unknown god. During that period of my agony, Lord Jesus intervened and revealed Himself to me through His servant and filled me with the baptism of the Holy Spirit.

Imbued with Power on High

The baptism of the Holy Spirit with outward evidence of speaking in tongue imbued me with power from on high over demonic spirits (Acts 1:8).

THE POWER OF THE INVISIBLE FORCES

Can Christians have demons in them? We read this in Mark 1:23–26:

> And there was in their synagogue a man with an unclean spirit; and he cried out, saying, let us alone what have we to do with thee, thou Jesus of Nazareth? art thou come to destroy us? I know thee who thou art, the Holy One of God. And Jesus rebuked him, saying, hold thy peace, and come out of him. And when the unclean spirit had torn him, and cried with a loud voice, he came out of him.

A man in a synagogue, apparently, was a Jew; and he was worshipping the true God in the synagogue. But when Jesus was there, the demons could not withstand the Holy One, and they knew who Jesus was and they were afraid. All those years, they lived inside of that man and operated in and through him, but they were exposed. Jesus did not communicate or bargained with them but rebuked them and commanded them to shut their mouth and to come out of that man. The unclean spirits convulsed the man and cried out with a loud voice and came out of him.

When the person is born again and is spirit filled, their spirit man regenerates and the unclean spirit, the demonic spirit, will not operate through their spirit man. They attach themselves into their soul and operate in them and through them, through their souls. Our thoughts, imaginations, emotions, and minds are part of our soul. It is, therefore, crucial and important to keep our minds, thoughts, and imaginations with the Word of God, to be on the guard of negative thoughts and negative feelings and to replace it with the promise of God and to walk in the spirit.

When we keep our soul in line with the word of God, we have the upper hand and authority over the unclean spirits so that they have to obey us when we command them with the authority of the word of God, and with the power of the Holy Spirit, and in the Name of Jesus.

– 17 –
Testimonies

HEALED OF THE DAMAGED ANKLE

The first day of my theology school at ORU, as I was getting out of the school, I felt like someone pushed me. So fell from the top of the stairs and landed at the bottom. My shoe heal came out and my right ankle was twisted. I was in severe pain. My feet was swollen and turned into blue. Then one of my friends, who was a physician recommended me to go to the hospital. I decided not to go to the hospital or to see any doctors but to stand on the Word of God. I could not put shoes, but I wore only socks and started to speak the Word over my ankle and my feet in the Name of Jesus. By God's grace in a weeks time all the swelling had gone and the color came back to normal. I was totally healed by the authority of the Word of God.

HEALED BY THE AUTHORITY OF THE WORD OF GOD AND BY THE POWER OF THE WORD

I was to attend the Clergy's meeting in December. We had only one car at that time. So my daughter was driving the car to her office and from there I was to take the car. She got out and about to enter her office building and turned to say buy to me. At that time she saw me on the ground with the pool of blood. As I was getting out of the passenger's seat to go to the driver's seat I slipped because of the ice and fell flat on my face. My lip was cut inside. She came running and took me in the car and I asked her to take me home. Those who came to see me said that I need to go to the doctor and there might be concussion. So the fear started coming. So I sent all of them out and closed the door and stood in front of the mirror and spoke to my lips and to my body to come in line with the Word of God and applied the Blood of the Lamb over my lips and my brain and covered myself with the Blood of the Lamb. Glory to Jesus the very next day as though some one stitched my lips and I was totally healed.

Oman

I was thrown out of a bathtub and my head was banged to the toilet seat as I was showering before going to church to preach the Gospel. The Lord protected me as nothing happened to me. I knew the enemy was upset that he tried to prevent me from preaching the Gospel. Many healings took place that afternoon, and people got healed of the migraine headache as well.

Muslim Girl

One Muslim girl was tormented by an evil spirit. For the longest time, she suffered from headache, and an unseen creature used to pull her leg at night that she could not sleep. She was a soothsayer. They went to different doctors—witch doctors, temples, Muslim mullahs, and spent lot of money—but found no remedy. After I was baptized in the Holy Spirit, I informed that Muslim girl that I found out the remedy for her problem.

She was living with her brother. I asked them if they have anything brought from the witch doctors, temples, and mosques. Sure enough, they had coconut, ashes, and so many things in their house. I asked them to throw everything outside the house, which they did. I then shared the Gospel, had her renounce the soothsayer, and told her to ask forgiveness for all the things she was involved. I then led both of them to the Lord and rebuked the evil spirits to get out of her life and not to come back again in the Jesus's name.

From that day on, she was totally set-free. I handed the Bible and instructed her, in order to maintain her healing, she has to read the Bible and to follow the Lordship of Jesus. From that day on, she was completely healed of her headache, and the unseen creature pulled her leg at night no more. She was totally healed and delivered by the power of the Holy Spirit and by the authority of the word of God and in the name of Jesus.

Since they were Muslims, they could not admit that they embraced Jesus as their Lord in public. They had to hide the Bible in their home. I frequently went to their house and taught them. The previous night before I could go to their house, I saw in my dream a huge black bull chasing me with such ferocity; on the other side, a big crowd was watching me and they were afraid that I would be attacked by that bull. By then, I stood there and, with my finger pointing out at the bull, commanded it to get out in the name of Jesus; and it turned around and left. It was the sign for me of the victory in Jesus's name. Sure enough, as I saw in my dream, Jesus gave me the victory and won those two Muslims to the kingdom of God.

Sri Lankan Couple

God gave me an opportunity to minister to one Sri Lankan couple. The husband had a good job, and they had a maidservant. In the meantime, he developed a relationship with the maid and harassed his wife to go back to Sri Lanka. The wife had planned on going back to Sri Lanka because of her husband's pressure.

One of his cousins informed me and the local pastor about it and asked us to pray for them. So that pastor and I went to their house to pray for the family. When we went, he was upstairs but refused to come down for prayer. We then ministered to the wife and encouraged her not to leave him and prayed with her. After the prayer we were about to leave the house, but by then he came down and asked for forgiveness because he started vomiting blood and he got scared of his own death. We then prayed with him, and he reconciled with his wife. God intervened in his life and broke the power of the enemy.

A Toy of Mask Face

One little girl of six years old had a high temperature. When I went to their house to pray for that little girl, my eyes went into a toy mask lying on the floor. So I asked the mother from where they got the mask. I told them that that needs to be removed from their house and be thrown out. The mother said that it was a gift given to that little girl by one of their colleagues who went on vacation to Indonesia. Once that mask had been removed from the house, I prayed for te child for protection and bound the forces of the darkness in the name of Jesus. And the child became completely well then and there.

Some people have no idea as to how the spirits are operating through articles, toys, antiques, etc. They are innocent and they think it is a toy or a decorative item and they bring it home. Our innocence does not stop the demonic spirits from operating through those items. When we buy stuff, especially from overseas, we must seek God's protection.

Decorative Buddha's Face

One time we were having a prayer meeting in one of a newly converted believer's house. As we were praying, the Lord showed me that there was something in their house that opened the door to the demonic spirit to come in. So we stopped the prayer and looked around their house. As we looked around, I saw the decorative Buddha's face in their hallway. I mentioned the Buddha needed to be removed and destroyed. Accordingly, they removed it and destroyed. I took authority over the forces of darkness that came through that item in the name of Jesus and pleaded the blood of Jesus over that house in the name of Jesus. We then felt the presence of the Lord during our prayer time.

Freedom from Demonic Possession

In 1995, I was ministering in India in a crusade meeting. At the end of the meeting, as I was praying for the people, one woman lifted her hands and said, "Hallelujah, hallelujah." So the local pastor, the one who was interpreting for me, tapped her head and asked her, "Who is it?" She replied, "Satan, Satan." She was profusely started sweating. I then took authority over that demon and cast him out of her in Jesus's name. She came under the power of God and fell on the floor. When she got up, she was completely healed of all her diseases and sicknesses by the power of the Holy Spirit.

A Woman Oppressed of the Devil

In 1987, I shared the Gospel of Jesus Christ in one of the Spirit Filled Assemblies of God Church in India. At the end of the sharing, many people came forward for healing and had been touched by the Lord. As I was leaving, one lady approached me and requested me to pray for her healing. She complained of headache, so I invited her to come to my place the following day.

The following day, she came to my place. To my surprise, as I laid my hand on her and pleaded the blood of the Lamb, she fell on the floor. When she got up, her head started turning round and round, nonstop. In the meantime, she asked me to give her a water to drink. So I gave her the water to drink. I had no idea, at that time, but I was not supposed to give her the drink. It was not her, but the demon wanted to drink. She then told me that sometime while she was cooking, the evil spirit would manifest and she would collapse. It went on for a long time, nearly two hours, but she was not set-free. I had no clue. I thought she was having headaches. I then sent her home and told her that I would contact her.

In the meantime, I found out the pastor involved in the deliverance ministry and I contacted him. He then brought with him one of his associates, and three of us prayed over her. She was a female, but during the time of prayer, the demon spoke with a male voice. She was a born-again and spirit-filled Christian, but the demon was operating in her life in her soul. It took nearly five hours, but she was then set-free by the authority of the word of God and in the name of Jesus and by the power of the Holy Spirit.

THE POWER OF THE INVISIBLE FORCES

Worshipper of Khali Set-Free

In 1988, I was ministering in one of the Assembly of God churches in India. There was one Hindu convert who asked for prayer for her knee, and while I was praying, she felt like someone hammered her head. She felt the severe pain. In other words, the demon was not happy. I then rebuked that demon out of her life in Jesus's name and by the power of the Holy Spirit. She was then totally healed.

The following day, she brought one of her friend, a Khali worshipper, to the church for prayer. As I started praying for that person, her tongue grew and came out of her mouth, so long that I was myself amazed to see such a manifestation of the devil. I then cast that demon out of her life in the name of Jesus and by the authority of the word of God. She was then set-free by the power of the Holy Spirit. I then asked her to renounce the goddess Khali and all other gods and goddesses in Jesus's name. I led her to the Lord and advised her to stay close to the Lord and to read the Word of God and to stay away from the old ways. Her countenance had been changed, and she was totally set-free by the power of the Holy Spirit.

Freedom from Witchcraft

In 1998, I was having a healing seminar in one of the churches in India. After the morning session, the church was catering lunch, and the people were having lunch. Just then, one well-dressed Hindu lady came to me and said that someone cast a curse on her for her to die in a month's time. I then broke the power of that curse off her. She came under the power of God and started crawling on the floor like a snake. I then broke the power of the python off her, and I loosed the Spirit of God and the blood of Jesus upon her life in Jesus's name. When she got up, she was totally set-free. I then led her to the Lord and instructed her to get rid of all the idols from her house and to worship the living God through Jesus Christ. If not, those demons would return and she would be in trouble. I also encouraged her to read the Bible.

Free from Pornography Addiction

In 2000, I was having a healing service in one of the churches in India. People brought a man to be prayed over. He was an IT guy working in America and had a good status and a well-paying job. He became insane and unable to function.

The Lord showed me the root cause of the problem (Matt. 6:22–23). I asked him if he was watching pornography. He did admit he was addicted to pornography, and the unclean spirit entered in to his body and took control of his mind. I asked him to ask the Lord to forgive him for his sin and asked him to renounce it in the name of Jesus. I then took authority over that evil spirit and cast him out in the name of Jesus. He was then totally set-free by the power of the Holy Spirit and by the authority of the word of God and by the power of the blood of Jesus.

Set-Free from the Spirit of Insanity

In 1993, as a team, we went to Mexico on a mission trip. In one of the crusade meetings, one woman who looked insane came for prayer. As I was about to lay my hand and pleaded the blood of Jesus, her head started spinning as though there were no bones in her neck. I then took authority in the word of God, and by the power of the Holy Spirit she was set-free.

That same evening, once the meeting was over, one young man came to me and started speaking in Spanish, showing his ears. By then, I could not find the translators, so I thought he was having ear problems. As I was about to put my hand on his ears to pray, by then, he fell on the floor and started crawling like a snake. I then took authority in the name of Jesus and by the authority of the word of God and by the power of the Holy Spirit. He was then set totally free. We were then told that he was the son of that insane woman who was delivered earlier. The following day, they brought the idols in their house, and we demolished those idols in the name of Jesus.

Baby in the Womb Came Back to Life

On one crusade meeting, one young six-month-pregnant woman came for prayer. Since she was pregnant, I prayed for the baby in the womb and for the mother and for the fullness of time for her to have a safe delivery in Jesus's name. She did not tell me her problem. But, praise God, the following day, she came and testified that her baby died in the womb and the doctor asked her to abort the baby. But she came for prayer, by faith in Jesus. She testified that her baby's heartbeat came back when I prayed, and she did not have to abort the baby.

Set-Free from the Incubus

In Oregon, one woman approached me for prayer. She was a born-again and spirit-filled Christian. She was witnessing for Jesus and had a passion for Jesus. She did not let anyone know what she was actually going through. She confided with me that at night, she was tormented and could not sleep because an incubus would come and have sex with her. I was utterly shocked when I heard that she was tormented by an incubus and having a sex with her. She needed to be delivered, and she requested me to help her. That was the day I travelled from Tulsa to Oregon. I was tired and I was not prepared for her deliverance. I told her that I would contact her and let her know when to meet.

I met her again, and she told me her life story. Both her parents were into drugs. She was about six years old, and her parents told her that they would take her to one of their relatives' house. So they took her to someone's house and left her there but never came back. She was then sent to different foster homes and ended up in drugs and prostitution. She got married to a drug addict. Finally, she got saved through an Evangelic meeting and set-free from drugs.

She had passion for Jesus and witnessed for Christ and loved the Lord, yet she had the problem of the incubus. I then met with her for few times and prayed with her and cast that incubus off her by the authority of the word of God and in the name of Jesus. She was then set-free totally by the authority of the word of God and in the name of Jesus and by the power of the Holy Spirit.

Set-Free from the Bondages

One man locked himself inside his room. No one was able to get him out of the room or communicate with him. God gave me an opportunity to talk to him. He was able to communicate with me and was able to confide with me. He had killed his father and was seeing his father every night chasing him in his dream. He was petrified and was unable to move out of his room. I then shared the story of Moses and of King David as to how they both were murderers and yet God forgave them when they admitted their mistakes and asked for forgiveness. He then repented of his sin and asked God to forgive him of his sin. I then led him to the Lord and cast the demon off him by the authority of the word of God and in the name of Jesus. He was then set-free from the bondage and was able to come out and was able to work with others.

Free from Psychic Power

A woman at a mental hospital underwent shock treatment for her mental illness. The psychiatric treatment is like a Band-Aid with no cure. She was born again and spirit filled. She admitted that she watched the show in TV and contacted the psychic for consultation. That opened the door for the unseen evil spirits to invade her mind. Once the unseen forces get access to a person's mind, they will then control the will of that person as well. I asked her to renounce the psychic power. I also told her to ask for forgiveness from Lord Jesus. Once she did that, I closed the door that opened to the psychic power in the name of Jesus. I prayed for her to have the sound mind in Jesus's name. She was then completely set-free and healed of her mind.

Sex Offender

I ministered to a sex offender. He was molested by his own father when he was four years old. Once he became an adult, he got married, and he then in turn molested his very own son at the age of four. It is the spirit running in the family. Unless we break the power of that spirit in the mighty name of Jesus, and by the power of the blood of Jesus, and by the authority of the word of God, and by the power of the Holy Spirit—it would continue to operate in the family. Unfortunately, in that facility, I was not permitted to address that demon and cast that demon out of his life.

It is really sad that they don't allow the Spirit of God to move on those people. They simply drug them with no result.

Set-Free from Demonic Possessions

Another guy I ministered to was fully possessed by a demon. He had tattoos of witches and dragons all over his body. When the spirit of anger would come, no one could tame him. They had to tie him to the bed. He was coming from a Mormon background. Before he could be put in this facility, two pastors from their Mormon temple came to deliver him to his house. But when the demon manifested, they ran away, it seems.

One fine day, the Lord gave me an opportunity to talk to him. He used to watch some of the Christian channel in the TV. He wanted to know why the preachers are pushing the people to the ground, so he asked the chaplain in his unit. She said, "I know someone who can explain it to you." She told me and asked permission from their supervisor for me to go with her to that unit. I explained to him it was the power of God causing the people to go down and not the preachers pushing them. He then told me of his experience as to how the demons would appear to him and how, at times, the demons drove his truck. Sometime, the demon appeared to him in the form of a beautiful woman.

I asked him what was his childhood was like. He told me at age six, he witnessed his father shot and killed in front of his eyes. Then his mother could not afford to take care of him and put him in a foster home. He was then sent from foster homes to foster home and were given hand-me-downs and suffered greatly. As he grew up, he went into drugs, alcohol, and women. He then became violent and stabbed someone. As a result, he was sentenced to prison, and from prison, he was then transferred to a mental hospital. He was sentenced for twenty years.

I shared with him the Gospel and asked him if he wants to be free. Praise God, he agreed. When I started praying and casting the demons out of his life, in the name of Jesus, the demon manifested. It took over two hours, and then he coughed a big, black-colored piece of meat, which flew out of his mouth. Then his countenance totally changed, and he was totally set-free. I then led him to the Lord and asked him to renounce the drugs, alcohol, and women. I then prayed for his inner healing and prayed for him for the infilling of the Holy Spirit. Glory to Jesus! Although he was sentenced for twenty years, he was then released in nine months, period. He was totally discharged and was not even asked to report to a halfway house.

When he was discharged, I was in another state. After a few years, I went back to his state on a mission trip. He then became my driver and drove me to different churches and to Bible school and gave a testimony.

He divorced his Mormon wife. He had one girl and two boys. But once he was set-free, he witnessed to his ex-wife, and she committed her life to the Lord. When I went on a mission trip to his state, the Lord made a way for me to remarry them and prayed for the baptism of the Holy Spirit for his wife and the daughter. They both were baptized with the Holy Spirit.

Once he was discharged, I advised him to enroll to a Bible school, but he decided to take up a position as a truck driver and decided to fulfill his duties toward his family. After a few years, he had passed away. In the last stage of his life, when he was in the hospital, his wife asked me to be there, so I went and did his funeral. At the funeral, many people shared their testimony of his witness to them.

Set-Free from a Religious Spirit

One woman came to me to be prayed for. She loved the Lord, was strong in the Lord, and had been baptized with the Holy Spirit. Her husband and all her family were Catholics. Before she accepted the Lord, she also practiced Catholicism. I then took authority over that religious spirit and cast that demon out of her in the name of Jesus and by the power of the Holy Spirit. As I was ministering, she started vomiting, and then she was totally set-free.

Healed of Cervical Cancer

One lady was healed and delivered of her heart problem during the women's meeting in the West Coast. Later on, once I came home, I received a phone call. It was that lady who received her healing. She said that her daughter was suffering from cervical cancer and that she was scheduled for surgery. She therefore asked for prayer. So I prayed with her over the phone and rebuked that cervical cancer and commanded that cervical cancer to get off her daughter's body, in the name of Jesus. What God has not planted cannot exist in her body, in Jesus's Name.

I then prayed for her for the infilling of the Holy Spirit. She was beautifully filled with the Holy Spirit with an outward sign of speaking in an unknown tongue. I then told her to take one more x-ray before she could do the surgery. Accordingly, they took her daughter for an x-ray, but the X-ray came out negative. They thought something was wrong with that X-ray machine. So they took another x-ray from another machine, and that machine also showed the X-ray as negative. Then the doctor certified for her daughter as free of cervical cancer. She then had her second child. Now, that child is thirteen years old, and her mother was free of cervical cancer once and for all. Thanks be to Jesus.

Unforgiveness-Caused Arthritis

One hospice patient's family member had severe arthritis. He could not use his hands and knees. He was in severe pain. I shared with him the Gospel and asked him if he has any unforgiveness toward anyone. He admitted that he was holding a grudge and unforgiveness toward his ex-wife. I asked him to forgive her so that he will be healed, but he refused to forgive his ex-wife. He preferred to be sick rather than forgive his ex-wife.

God has given us the choice to make; it is up to an individual. Deuteronomy 30:19 says, "I have set before you life and death, blessing and cursing, therefore choose life that both thou and thy seed may live."

Healed from Vomiting Blood

In one of the Assemblies of God churches in Houston, one woman was very sick, vomiting blood. That woman saw me in her dream even before I could go to Houston. She saw me in her dream praying in the name of Jesus and that she got healed. The pastor of that church took me to her house to pray for her. In her house was one picture on the wall. I did not feel good about it. I asked her from where she got that picture. She replied that it was given to her by her brother, who is in Mexico. She admitted that he was involved in witchcraft. I told her that the picture needed to be destroyed, which she did. After that, I prayed with her, and I broke every curse, witchcraft power, and demonic forces off her, in the name of Jesus. I loosed the healing power of Jesus over her life, in the name of Jesus and by the authority if the word of God. She was then completely healed, and from that day on, she did not vomit blood any more.

Hospice Patient Healed from Liver Cancer

One patient in the hospice had liver cancer. He was in the last stage of cancer, and the doctor said he had less than a week to live. He was passing blood in his stool. He was diabetic, and both his legs from the knee down were amputated. He was a Catholic, and his wife was a Baptist. His wife wanted him to live, and he also wanted to live. I saw their faith and told them, "If you believe, I will pray that he will live." They both agreed.

I led him to the Lord and prayed with him. I commanded the cancer in his body to die and to wither in Jesus's name. What God has not planted cannot exist in his body, in Jesus's name. I then asked the Lord to pour out His healing power from the top of the man's head and to the soles of the man's feet, in Jesus's name. I then gave the healing scriptures to his wife to pray over him three to four times a day because he did not have the strength to say the scriptures. He was like a bedridden skeleton, and his family were preparing for his funeral. In the hospice, there were no medicine as such, except for painkillers.

In the meantime, he developed herpes around his waist. His wife called me at 3:00 a.m. and started crying that he had high fever. I prayed with her over the phone, and the next morning, I went to their house and prayed over him and cursed that herpes to die in Jesus's name. Glory to Jesus, the very next day, that herpes was dried and vanished. His appetite improved, and he was able to eat and started putting on weight. He was then able to get up from his bed, and started loading the dishwasher, and started moving around his yard, and started watering the plants. He admitted to the hospice in February 1998, and in October 1998, they found no cancer. He was then discharged from the hospice. No doctors could take the credit for his healing but the Lord, who healed him completely and restored his health.

Set-Free from Oppression

In 2000, I went on a mission trip to Swaziland. The pastor who invited me mentioned that there was no problem for the accommodation. The accommodation was provided by one of their church members' house. We went to see that house had a small room that my suitcase would not fit in. Moreover, the next-door neighbor had her radio playing loudly. So I told the pastor that I could not stay in that place. I then asked him to find an accommodation that I would pay.

He then took me to a place where there was a very small heater, and that heater was only allowed to be turned on for a couple of hours. It was cold, and I did not take any warm clothes with me. I told the Lord that I didn't want to die there in the cold.

The next morning, at breakfast, the hospital officials were also having breakfast. One of the hospital nurse conversed with me and offered me a place in her accommodation. She had a big place. She accommodated me and gave me one of her rooms to stay. As a result, I was able to stay there for a whole month and ministered to the locals, especially to women who were oppressed and suppressed because of their culture. Their culture was such that any man could marry any number of wives but any woman cannot. Moreover, the women had to work and raise the kids and the men would not lift a finger. Men could divorce his wife, but the women cannot divorce her husband. Additionally, men have to be given the best food.

Moreover, even among Christians, their culture was such that they would have a *sibaya* (kraal) behind their houses to consult the ancestral spirit, especially during weddings and when new babies were born. They would consult and receive the blessing from their ancestral spirit. According to biblical principle, this practice is forbidden. I shared the Word of God against their cultural practice of ancestral spirit worship and polygamy. On the other hand, I shared and introduced the culture according to biblical principle.

In the morning, I ministered to the local women in the house. In the afternoon, the pastor took me to the hospitals to pray for the sick, and in the evenings I ministered at the tent meetings.

Blood Covering

I was on the phone with one of my prayer partners, and as I was talking, I was thrown out from one end to the other and my head was banged to the wall. I then took authority and bound the forces of the darkness and covered myself and the place where I lived with the blood of Jesus.

Set-Free from Tormenting Spirits

The Swaziland king's brother was in the hospital, almost dying. The pastor took me to the hospital. The king's brother told me that he was oppressed, tormented, and had nightmares caused by the evil spirits. He was so afraid, he could not sleep. He graduated from Kentucky University. I ministered to him and led him to the Lord. I then took authority over the demons and prayed with him. Since that day, he was able to sleep, and he was totally set-free.

An Ear Healed

In Swaziland, in one of the meetings, they brought a young boy whose ear was leaking. They took him to several doctors, but there was no cure. I laid my hands on his ears and rebuked the spirit afflicting his ear to come out in Jesus's name and commanded his ear to come in line with the word of God, in Jesus's name. Glory to Jesus, his ear became perfectly normal, and there was no more leakage from that boy's ear. He was totally healed by the authority of the word of God and by the power of the Holy Spirit.

Set-Free from Another Demonic Spirit

I was ministering in the East Coast. One woman came to me to be prayed for. She complained of knee pain, and she wanted me to pray for her knee. She is a Born-Again, spirit-filled, and a wonderful Christian.

Before I could pray for her, I prayed in tongue, and the Lord showed me that there was a problem in the umbilical cord with her mother. I barely mentioned about the umbilical cord with her mother, and she rolled her eyes and came to hit me with such rage that the woman in the house pulled her down in her collar. I then realized it was demon, and I took authority with the word of God and cast the demon out of her, in the name of Jesus. She was then set-free.

After that, I prayed for her knee, and her knee was healed. She then cried and apologized that she didn't mean to hit me but that something came over her and she lost her control.

Set-Free from Witchcraft

One young kid of four years old was disturbed by the image of an old man coming from his window every night. He could not sleep and would go to his parents' room every night, crying. They did not know what to do. In the meantime, one Indonesian pastor informed me the situation and asked me to go with him to pray for that kid. The child's mother was Asian, and she confided that she went to a witch doctor who told her that she would have a boy and specified the birthmark her child would have. Sure enough, she had her boy, and he had a birthmark, as the witch doctor said.

First of all, I led her to the Lord. I then told her to ask for forgiveness from the Lord and to renounce her involvement with the witch doctor. I then asked her to clean her house, and she removed all the items not pleasing in the eyes of the Lord. I then prayed a deliverance prayer with her child. I anointed their house, and since then, her kid has no problems and is able to sleep well at night.

Free from Invisible Evil Spirits

The Indonesian pastor took me to another household who were used to experiencing paranormal activities in their apartment. As I was presenting the Gospel to the couple, all of a sudden, the big clock fastened to the wall was thrown out and fell on the floor further away. It was the sign that the evil spirit did not want them to hear the Gospel. I then took authority over the evil spirits by the authority of the word of God, and by the power of the Holy Spirit, and by the power of the blood of Jesus, and in the name of Jesus. The demons cannot stand before the name of Jesus and the blood of Jesus. From that day on, they did not have any demonic problems.

Set-Free from Gluttony

In the East Coast, as I was ministering in one of the Assemblies of God churches, after preaching, I was praying for one woman. Her stomach started to bloat out, and the Lord showed me that it was the spirit of gluttony. As I broke the power of the spirit of gluttony and commanded it to get off her, in Jesus's Name, she was totally set-free and got healed by the authority of the word of God, and in the name of Jesus, and by the power of the Holy Spirit.

Healed from Demonic Oppression

I was invited to speak at the Christ Church Women's Conference in Tulsa. After I finished speaking, I called the people to come for prayer. One woman came for her headache to be healed. I prayed for her, and her headache was gone. But as she went back to her seat, her headache returned in a big way.

She came back for prayer, and that time, my eyes went into her necklace. I asked her where she bought her necklace. She said that she bought her necklace from an antique store. It had a demonic attachment to it. I told her to remove her necklace, which she did. I then broke the power of the darkness off her, in Jesus's name, and prayed with her and covered her with the blood of Jesus. She was then completely healed of her headache once and for all, in the name of Jesus.

Set-Free from Horoscopes

I was ministering to the people in a home setting, and the Lord directed me to a woman and gave me a word of knowledge that she was involved in reading and believing in horoscope. I asked her, and she was surprised as to how I knew. She was suffering from pain in different parts of her body and was full of fear.

While I was praying, the demonic spirit manifested, and both her legs started twisting. I then took authority over that demonic spirit by the authority of the word of God, and in the name of Jesus, and by the power of the Holy Spirit. I asked her to renounce the reading of the horoscope and all such activities. She did so, and then she was totally healed and set-free.

Full-Blown AIDS

One patient was very sick with full-blown AIDS. He was a very young, tall, and handsome guy. He was prostituting and got himself AIDS. I led him to the Lord, and while confessing his sin to the Lord, he cried out loudly like a child. He repented of his sin and submitted himself to the Lordship of Jesus. I then ministered to him, covered him from the top of his head to the soles of his feet with the blood of Jesus, and broke the power of the darkness off him, in Jesus's name. I asked the Lord to reach out and touch him with His healing power. The following day, he went to be with the Lord.

Cardiac Patient

One young patient was admitted to a hospital in the cardiac unit. He was a drug addict. The day he was admitted. I tried to see him as a hospital chaplain, but he refused to see me. In the meantime, I told him, "If you need me anytime, I will be there for you," and I left.

The following day, he himself asked for me because he was scared since the doctor had mentioned that his heart would stop at any moment. So I went to see him. I led him to the Lord and I prayed with him. He was then transferred to ICU, and he had asked for me again in ICU. I went and encouraged him in the Lord. He wanted to live, but he then went into a coma. I went and ministered to him, even when he was in coma. The person might be in a coma and their flesh may not be moving, but their spirit man is well and aware what is going on. On the third day of his coma, he went to be with the Lord.

Healed of Incest and Sexual Activities

One young person came to me for a spiritual counseling. She was in her thirties. She was sexually molested by her own father from a very early age. Her mother knew about it but did not pay attention. Later on, she got married, but her marriage did not last long. She emotionally and mentally struggled and suffered. She approached the pastor for help, but that pastor told her to confess the word of God so she would be healed. She did so, but it was no use. She still suffered.

I provided her the spiritual counseling and prayed with her. It took a few sessions, but she was then healed of all the wounds and hurt, by the power of the Holy Spirit and by the authority of the word of God. She was then able to forgive her father and mother. Her mother was a very reserved and prideful person. But when she saw the change in her daughter, she volunteered to come to me for counseling. I counseled to her mother. Once she received her freedom, by the power of the Holy Spirit and by the authority of the word of God, she recommended her sister, who came and had been healed of the past hurts and wounds, by the power of the Holy Spirit and by the authority of the word of God. Thus, the entire family had been set-free.

A Deaf Ear Healed

In India, in Chennai, during one healing service, a little boy was born deaf and his parents brought him forward for prayer. I put my hand on that little boy's ear and commanded the dumb and deaf spirit to come out of him, in the name of Jesus, and I spoke his ear to function normally in Jesus's name. Glory be to God, that little boy's ear was opened and he was able to hear, right then and there. Jesus never prayed for the sick but rebuked and commanded the demonic spirit to come out. He has given us the power of attorney to use the name of Jesus. To that name of Jesus, every knee has to bow and every tongue has to confess that He is the Lord.

An Adulterous Child Healed

One woman came to me for spiritual counseling. She needed help with her son, who was so full of rage that no one could tame him. I asked her about her delivery experience. She then confided with me that her child was not from her husband but was born out of wedlock through one of his colleagues. She did not disclose it to anyone, including her husband. In other words, her child was born breaking God's covenant of marriage.

When we break God's covenant, it opens the door to Satan to come in and to destroy us. I asked her to plead mercy and ask for forgiveness from the Heavenly Father. That closed the door that had been opened to the enemy, by the power of the blood of Jesus. Simultaneously, I took authority over her son, by the authority of the word of God, and in the name of Jesus, and by the power of the Holy Spirit.

- 18 -

The Power and Authority Over Invisible Forces of Darkness

The New Testament speaks of God's power and authority in these verses:

> And when He had called His twelve disciples to Him, He gave them power over unclean spirits, to cast them out, and to heal all kinds of sickness and all kinds of disease. Go, preach, saying, the kingdom of heaven is at hand. Heal the sick, cleanse the lepers, raise the dead, cast out demons. Freely you have received, freely give. (Matt. 10:1, 7–8)

> After these things The Lord appointed other seventy also, and sent them two and two before his face into every city and place whither he Himself would come. And the seventy returned again with joy, saying, Lord, even the devils are subject unto us through thy Name. And He said unto them, I beheld Satan as lightning fall from heaven. Behold, I give unto you power to tread on serpents and scorpions and over all the power of the enemy and nothing shall by any means hurt you. (Luke 10:1, 17–21)

THE POWER OF THE INVISIBLE FORCES

And these signs will follow those who believe: in My (Jesus) name they will cast out demons. (Mark 16:17)

– 19 –

Conclusion

Romans 8:14 says, "For as many as are led by the Spirit of God, these are sons of God." The invisible power of God is in the word of God. In the invisible power of God, the invisible power of the devil tremble and fear. The word of God has the supreme authority upon the earth. To be spiritually prepared for Satan's attack, we must not only be baptized in the Holy Spirit, but we must also remain full of the Spirit. As children of God, we must live being led by the Spirit of God on a daily basis.

Authority and power is not of the flesh, not of natural weapons, or not armor but the spoken word of God. The power of God comes out of our mouth by the spoken word of God. The word of God has the supreme authority upon the earth. Jesus confronted and took authority over Satan by speaking the Word of God. With just one word from His lips, Jesus cast the demon out of people's lives. Everywhere Jesus went, He confronted the power of the enemy with the spoken Word and destroyed Satan's strongholds in the lives of the people.

God has given the same power and authority to the followers of Christ to confront Satan by speaking His Word and destroy his strongholds and conquer Satan in the power and authority of the Holy Spirit. Jesus has given His believers the power of attorney to use His name. To that name above every name, every knee has to bow and every tongue has to confess that Jesus is the Lord. Satan trembles at that name. Moreover, Satan is afraid of the Blood of Jesus. Believers have the authority and power to plead the blood of the

Lamb. Jesus has equipped the believers with the power and authority with the infilling of the Holy Spirit with the power of attorney to use His name and His Blood.

John 10:10 says, "The thief cometh not, but for to steal, and to kill, and to destroy: I am come that they might have life, and that they might have it more abundantly." Here, Jesus made it very clear that Satan is the one who steals, kills, and destroys the human beings. Jesus, on the other hand, is the one who heals, restores, and gives abundant life.

So Jesus promised us in His Word, "Verily, verily, I say unto you, he that believeth on Me, the works that I do shall he do also, and greater works than these shall he do because I go unto My Father" (John 14:12).

REFERENCES

Cerullo, Morris. *God's Victorious Army Bible, Spiritual Warfare Edition—Spiritual Warfare Commentaries by Morris Cerullo.* Morris Cerullo World Evangelism, 1988.

Schamback, R. W. *Demon Possession Today & How to Be Free.* Schambach Revivals, Inc., 1992.

Sumrall, Dr. Lester. *101 Questions & Answers on Demon Powers.* South Bend: Lester Sumrall Evangelistic Association, 1983.

ABOUT THE AUTHOR

GLADYS WAS BORN IN India and lived in the Middle East, in Oman, for sixteen years. She left her job in 1990 and totally committed her life to serving the Lord.

She pioneered the Women's Aglow Fellowship in Oman and ministered to people of diverse cultures. She has travelled extensively around the world, preaching the Gospel of Jesus Christ and conducting healing seminars. She is an interdenominational ordained minister. She is an Evangelist, teacher, and a professional chaplain. The gifts of the Holy Spirit are operating in her ministry.

Her educational background includes a master's degree in missions from Oral Roberts University and board-certified chaplain training at Oregon Psychiatric State Hospital. She attended Morris Cerullo Ministry School, Billy Graham School of Evangelism, the Institute in Basic Life Principles, and Christian Family Institute.

She has served as a hospice chaplain and bereavement coordinator in Houston, Texas, and a staff chaplain in Fresno, California. Currently, as a traveling minister, she travels around and conducts healing seminars, teaching and preaching the Gospel and setting the captives free by the power of the Holy Spirit.